LEARNING TO SAY GOODBYE

Learning To Say Goodbye

Dealing with Death and Dying

by Rosalie Peck, M.S.W., A.C.S.W.
and Charlotte Stefanics, R.N., C.S., Ed.D.

ACCELERATED DEVELOPMENT INC.
Publishers

Muncie,   Indiana

LEARNING TO SAY GOODBYE

Dealing with Death and Dying

Library of Congress Number: 87-70820

International Standard Book Number: 0-915202-71-9

2   3   4   5   6   7   8   9   10

 **ACCELERATED DEVELOPMENT INC.**
Publishers
3400 Kilgore Avenue
Muncie, IN 47034

DEDICATION

— from Rosalie

When I was a child dreaming dreams of becoming,
my parents allowed no one to scoff at my dreaming.
Rather, they encouraged me to believe in myself;
to embrace the concept of persistence; the
foundation that makes dreams come true.

To my parents, the late
James and Octavia Peck,
this book is, with love
and appreciation, dedicated.

— from Charlotte

Appreciation is expressed to my dear family in a
very special way; as through them I learned about
love, pain, suffering and joy which, after all, comprise
the process of life. The quality of our lives was and is
intensified through the knowledge that one day we will
be separated through death. We consequently learned
not to inhibit our lives through fear of death, but to
live each moment to its fullest.

Specifically, I acknowledge love and appreciation
to:
George Stefanics - my father who is deceased.
Mary Stefanics - my mother.
My sisters Ethel and her husband George Vance;
Mary Alvira and her husband Cornel Somogy; and
my brother Jesse Stefanics and his wife Mary
Louise.

ACKNOWLEDGEMENTS
— from Rosalie —

Writing is and has always been my greatest, my most compelling ambition. And so, I have been writing....about something and everything since I was a child having just learned to read. But to be published! This is the consumation of my deep desire to be a writer.

The process of becoming an author takes time. It is much like the process of discovering love, for, in each instance, the realization of having attained the elusive goal is a feeling of exquisite pleasure, tinged with a delightful touch of awe.

And so it is that I owe deep gratitude to many people who have helped me along the way. It would involve pages to individualize them all, but they know who they are. The following are incomparable:

Ms. Mary M. Kugleman, Ms. Pauline R. Tucker, and Ms. Mamie Doyle Brown, library assistant, Public Library, St. Petersburg, Florida. Their unselfish assistance and interest helped me to personify the wisdom of William R. Allen's truth that "research is to teaching what sin is to confession; without one, you have nothing to tell."*

My sincere thanks to the late Harold J. Greenier, M.D., and Luis M. Rodriguez, M.D., who offered consistent encouragement and provided valuable materials from their own private collection of books and articles for information and validation of certain medical references included here.

---

*William R. Allen, Quoted by Linda Dold Robinson "Gerontological Nursing Research" *Nursing and The Aged*, edited by Irene Mortenson Burnside, McGraw-Hill Book Co., 1976, p. 586.

I feel that all health care practitioners involved in terminal care are indebted to two major sources of inspiration who have served as beacons of light in an otherwise uncharted sea of darkness in human services. Dr. Cicely Saunders for her unequalled work at St. Joseph's Hospice, London, England, and Dr. Elisabeth Kubler-Ross for her outstanding work in death and dying.

My very special thanks to Ephraim who unselfishly helped me to help him experience his death.

Special thanks to my family and personal friends who have offered encouragement and support throughout these and other years. To Fred W. Alsup, M.D., for saving me from a clinical death; also for writing the introduction to this book, and for certain verifications of medical information included here.

To my special friend for having confidence in and patience with me during the development of *Learning to Say Goodbye*. To Marcia Silvera who did such a beautiful job preparing the manuscript. Many thanks to Charlotte Stefanics, my co-author, friend and colleague, whose personality, enthusiasm and special knowledge helped to make writing this book more exciting.

And finally, to George Jendrusiak, for listening and suggesting ideas for inclusion here, and for supporting my creative urgings; to Richard (Dick) Lloyd for his enthusiastic support of my ambitious efforts; to John O'Neill for helping me find the poetry; to Larry Badeaux for suggesting I write this book in the first place.

— from Charlotte

I am grateful to the many patients and their families with whom I have been involved as they experienced death and dying throughout my entire nursing career. Specifically, I refer to, and express appreciation to Community Hospital, Springfield, Ohio, where my role in terminal care evolved; and to Duke University School of Nursing, Durham, N.C., where I taught students the dynamics of loss and loneliness in caring for the terminally ill and their families.

CONTENTS

PREFACE

It is remarkable that after almost two hundred years as a death-denying society, Americans are now discussing death and dying so openly and with such forthright energy. We can be both amazed and proud of the progress we have made to lift the veil of mystery on a subject which was, until the early seventies, a topic to be avoided at all costs. Death was a subject that we steadfastly denied as the common denominator for all human life. It was a matter to be feared with such vigorous passion that the emotional burdens which inherently accompany death and the process of dying were significantly magnified. We can be proud of the progress made within the recent past to finally confront our fear and to become more enlightened in such a basic aspect of human life. This phenomenal development is leading to ever increasing public awareness, interest and concern for terminal patients and their families. We have progressed to the point of significant interest in thanatology, the study of death and the process of dying.

Material on death and dying is abundantly available. Books, articles, film strips, seminars, movies and television are providing copious information. These various resources are designed to meet the needs of our increasing fascination with the subject. The need is not in question. Still, there is the element of proper perspective in this new quest for knowledge on a very old and frightful subject. By this time, we are more aware of the grievous needs of people who are dying. We are beginning to recognize the dire needs of grieving families. More often we hear the term survivorship and how it relates in importance to total patient care. The crucial questions are: Who will provide these very sensitive services on a consistent basis? How does one learn to relate to dying patients on effective levels of competence? What is meant by therapeutic relationships with people for whom death is imminent? And, finally, what do you say to someone who is dying? In the process of establishing a supportive relationship with a person who is dying, whether that person is your patient, relative, or friend, you will at some point wonder, "But what about me? What is expected of me? Can I do it? How do I begin? Who can tell me how?" These are only a few of the many uncomfortable feelings and fears that are germane to the practical application of theoretical preparation for working with terminal patients. There is a vast difference between acquisition of theory and the moment when you and a dying person come face to face.

Learning to Say Goodbye is designed to provide a practical foundation for people who need relevant information to help them to cope with the emotional problems of death and dying. It contains much of the fundamental information that students of health care need to acquire and guidelines which practitioners who work with dying people also need to know and to have readily accessible. It is not a "how-to" book with mechanical solutions to herculean problems, but rather one that guides learning toward growth-producing development and away from the temptation to seek easy, formulaic solutions to difficult situations. *Learning to Say Goodbye* provides a pragmatic approach to an otherwise very difficult subject.

There is no household in the world that is not destined to keep multiple appointments with death. There are no magic situations to prevent death's coming, whether the occupants are rich or poor, young or old. Death comes because death *is*. Death is the equalizer in human affairs, without exception or partiality. The information included here is intended to encourage and assist you to learn more about yourself in relation to death and dying: how do you feel about death, not only the deaths of other people, but also your own? The manner in which you view and accept (or reject) your own mortality is the key to your understanding of your feelings, behaviors and attitudes toward death, and toward people who are dying.

It is not difficult to find resource materials on the kind of services that terminal patients need. It is more of a problem to find instructive information designed specifically to help you prepare yourself to meet the challenge of developing self-awareness, inner strengths and skills that are necessary for offering these unique, supportive services in terminal care.

It is expressly for these purposes that this book was written. While public attention is vigorously focused on care for people who are dying, attention must be realistically directed toward your need to acquire certain basic knowledge, insights, expectations and clarification of your own personal attitudes toward death and dying, things which are cruical to your individual effectiveness and well-being. This book is offered as a basic resource to help you discover and understand the scope of the problems, to realize their far-reaching implications, to help you learn to assess situations for yourself, and to discover how you can intervene with competence. *Learning to Say Goodbye* is designed to help you establish and maintain therapeutic relationships in terminal care and to feel better about yourself in the process.

Death is a natural phenomenon of life, but it is nevertheless a very difficult part of life's experiences. We are acutely aware of the needs of terminal patients and their families, but we are equally aware of the needs of people who provide special services to patients and families on a daily basis. Helping dying patients and their families is a special area of human interaction that demands the combination of high moral fibre, compassion, discipline and skills. It is often difficult and can be an emotionally draining experience. It can also be a highly gratifying experience, provided there are sufficient educational opportunities and support systems for staffs who provide these services. The basic prerequisite is education. With adequate foundation, the necessary skills can be achieved.

The development of this book was made considerably easier through the discovery that we mutually possess the following similiarities in our individual family backgrounds and attitudes toward death and dying. Specifically, we both feel that we have been aware of death all our lives; certainly we have been aware of life. And we were taught from early childhood by our respective parents to develop healthy attitudes of generous respect for life and death as natural phenomena stemming from the same source.

In our families, people die. They do not "pass" or "expire." We were taught that cars pass and insurance polices expire, but people die. Our shared philosophy of living and dying, therefore, is filled with an exuberant love of life as well as an abiding respect and understanding of death as a vital part of life. It is this shared philosophy which has inspired and enabled us to ultimately develop this book, which hopefully will help others who share the same outlook.

It is our hope that *Learning to Say Goodbye* will provide help, practical information, inspiration and guidelines to the general public, as well as to students and health care professionals who, having viewed film strips, read books and attended death and dying seminars and in-service training programs, confront the reality of death and still find themselves wondering, "but where do we go from here?"

FOREWORD

A wealth of books and articles pertaining to death and dying are available in our society today. Each publication has value, as it relates to a phenomenon that has for many years been a taboo subject in our country. This book, however, is different. *Learning to Say Goodbye* features a humanistic approach to death and dying and, to my knowledge, it is the first if not the only book of its kind. *Learning to Say Goodbye* provides information for dealing with the needs of the triad in health care systems which consist of the patient, the family and the staff. It further offers clearcut guidelines for establishing thanatology programs within health care facilities.

We physicians know that our goals are clearly defined: (1) to prevent disease; (2) to try to cure diseases; (3) to save lives. The reality of death is a paradox in this orientation, and when death occurs it is often viewed as a failure. We physicians, as humans, are intimately involved with death and dying and our attitudes toward death are molded throughout our medical training. Learning to come to terms with one's feelings about death is a gradual process. Death will never be a comfortable situation to confront for any of us. It is the most traumatic experience in life. As I see it, our challenge as physicians is to learn how to deal with the reality of death. To me this suggests the need for us to become involved with patients and their families, employing a humanistic approach which allows us to be supportive throughout the dying process.

Through continued educational efforts, as outlined in *Learning to Say Goodbye* we may be in the process of moving toward rediscovery of the value of human to human involvement in meeting our mutual needs in matters of death and dying. Within this process, we become aware of the essence of the here and now.

Fred W. Alsup, Ph.D., M.D.

INTRODUCTION

So live that when thy summons comes
To join the innumerable caravan
Which moves to that mysterious realm
Where each shall take his chamber
In the silent halls of death,
Thou go not like a quarry slave at night
Scourged to his dungeon
But sustained and soothed by an un-
faltering trust
Approach thy grave like one
Who wraps the drapery of his couch about
him
And lies down to pleasant dreams...
— *William Cullen Bryant[1]*

This meditative, thought-provoking composition, "Thanatopsis," was created by William Cullen Byrant when he was only 18 years old. It is a classic and considered to be among his best work. Once understood, it is never quite forgotten. The theme is death, yet the major thrust of the poem is the admonition to live a life of quality and to accept death with dignity. But what does that mean? What is a good death? And what is death with dignity? Perhaps it is the death that comes after a person succeeds in setting straight some of the unfinished aspects of his or her life; perhaps it means being able to ultimately accept death peacefully. Whatever it is, to accept death with dignity (peace) requires help from other people. The kind of help that encourages death with dignity requires emotional support from people who have a sincere, sensitive, concerned and dedicated commitment to comfort those who are dying. These are the people whose efforts gain respect and trust of terminal patients.

The old Negro spiritual, "I Want To Die Easy When I Die," suggests the desires of persons who, having lived around loved ones in familiar surroundings, die in the same setting with family and friends offering comfort and sharing a common grief. This must have been the "good death;" but we seldom experience that kind of death today. Most people, especially those suffering protracted terminal disease such as cancer, die in hospitals and nursing homes, frequently far from home and familiar faces and cared for by strangers who never knew them as healthy individuals with hopes and dreams and lives of their own.

Many people who have outlived family and friends have no one from the outside world who either knows or cares about them; but whether terminal patients are elderly, middle-aged, young adults or children, few of them die at home. Instead of family, friends and a trusted family physician, it is frequently up to strangers to help terminal patients and families to deal with the inherent stresses of death and the frightening process of dying. This development emphasizes the need for human services people to acquire the skills of offering appropriate and consistent supportive treatment to dying patients and, at the same time, to learn to cope with the stresses imposed upon the practitioner in the execution of these much needed services. Death is not an easy truth of life to cope with, nor will it ever be. And although there is an abundance of valid material written on the needs of terminal patients and families, not enough of it approaches the subject with a focus on the emotional needs of the practitioners who supply these services.

The level and quality of care provided to terminal patients and families is in direct proportion to the degree of comfort that people experience in the process of working with dying patients. Many students of the health professions have never experienced the death of a loved one, nor the emotional trauma that follows such a loss. In our society, death is traditionally one of the most frightening aspects of our lives. How then do we begin to learn to be effective in the holistic care and treatment of patients for whom death is imminent? Since we begin from a framework of zero to limited knowledge in this relatively untapped area of health care, what is required for caretakers to be effective in this specialized area of human service? Where do we begin? Let us first consider the process of learning:

Think back to the days when you were a baby and you were learning to walk. Remember those wobbly knees and how many times you fell? Remember the times that you landed on your face? And the more embarrassing times that you landed bottom first? Do you remember the skinned knees, the bruised elbows, the fright—the tears? Remember, too, that someone was usually there to lift you from your fall, to reassure and encourage you to get up and try again. Surely, you remember the moment that you began to need less help, when you fell less often as you began to discover your own individual center of gravity! Of course you remember the day that you stood all alone and walked independently to your heart's content! Remember the squeals of delight from your family and how proud you were! Oh...you don't remember...That was so long ago!

Then think back to the days when you were a baby and you were confidently walking about, going in whatever direction that suited you best at the moment. Recall the instant you discovered that not only could you walk, you could walk fast! You tried to walk faster and faster...and you fell. Remember the pain of the bruised lip? The bump on the head? And who was that someone who picked you up...again... reassured you again...and held your hand as you steadied yourself to try once more? Then one day you could walk fast...all alone...without falling! Recall the exhilarating feeling of confidence? Now, remember the day you walked so fast...and discovered that you could run. You learned to do these things because you had gone through a process, step by step.

Learning is a process that gradually unfolds itself like a blooming rose. The result is the acquisition of a body of knowledge attained through a combination of desire, motivation and effort; frustration and joy; trial and error; and most of all, persistence. Once learning has occurred, there is no need to recall the process of the task no matter how difficult it was. What counts is the result. Whether the experience is learning to walk, run, swim, dance, or bake a cake, the process is the same. Through the actual experience of doing, through trial and error, one day the goal becomes a reality.

Learning to work with terminal patients presents the same fundamental challenge, for it, too, is a process. In no way would you have learned to walk or to run by hearing instructions on how to move your feet or lift your knees. You had to experience the efforts, the fear of failure; the discomfort of feeling uncertain, inadequate and unprepared; the pain or embarrassment when you fell. These are the universal growing pains in the process of learning which cannot be avoided but which can be overcome.

What is ultimately acquired is the ability to apply skills which you already possess. Working effectively with terminal patients means the application of familiar skills developed to the highest level of your individual potential. Every person has his or her own unique style, and no two people will approach the same patient or problem in the same way. The secret of effectiveness lies within the acquired skill of the practitioner. Some babies, for instance, learn to walk with relatively little help while others require a great deal of assistance. The important thing is not the speed with which a child performs the task, but the ultimate acquisition of the skill. The same is true in learning to work with terminal patients and families. We already have the ability to talk to people, to establish rapport, identify problems, make assessments and seek solutions. We need to offer supportive treatment, to listen and encourage ventilation, the therapeutic relationship respects the values of catharsis; working within the problem-solving process, respecting confidentiality and allowing for individual differences. These needs are not new to us, they need only to be met. Learning how to intervene effectively comes through experiencing one's self when confronted with the dying person. This self awareness contributes to the body of knowledge and skills so necessary in helping people through the final experience.

Working therapeutically in terminal care requires specific knowlege in human behavior. It varies in degrees of complexity and is based firmly in the concept of individuality. Terminal patients are people who are "different" primarily in the sense that death is diagnostically anticipated. For this reason, their needs are of a more urgent nature. In other respects, they share problems that are common to any other patients. They too are concerned with issues relative to family and financial situations, and the difficulty of adjusting to hospitalization. To focus narrowly on the lethal aspect of a patient's situation would be like offering bread to one who is both hungry and thirsty.

PART I

HISTORICAL AND CULTURAL ATTITUDES TOWARD DEATH AND DYING

FEAR OF DEATH

What a wondrous thing it would be if the same energy that we invest in fear of death could be spent in exultation of life. (R. Peck)[2]

In America, where youth is cherished, sought after and embraced with feverish tenacity, age is not a popular topic of discussion because people fear the unattractive implications associated with growing old. In our society, youth is glorified through mass media which promotes perpetual beauty and youth while it negates the process of aging and the reality of death. It follows, therefore, that death is an even less popular subject because people fear dying and fear facing the known finalities and the unknown features of death.

Fortunately there is substantial evidence that these attitudes are finally beginning to undergo significant changes. This is evidenced by the proliferation of printed material, television and motion pictures as well as by academic involvement in teaching courses on death and dying. Death, as a part of life, has surfaced and is becoming a realty in terms of people's developing awareness of the emotional needs of dying patients and their survivors. As a result of these changes, the needs of caretakers who provide these services have also emerged for consideration.

Historically, death in America has been viewed as the greatest enemy of all mankind, And, while enemies are to be conquered, if the adversary cannot be vanquished, the result is that it becomes a hated thing, a terror to hide from, to fear, to escape, to deny, and, whenever possible, to ignore. The problem, then, is based not so much on death and what it is, as on death and how it is perceived.

Considerations of other culturistic attitudes toward death and dying may provide some insight into basic reasons for the differences in our own western fears and eastern acceptance of death as a natural part of life. In Japan, according to an observation by Schneidman, "the Japanese feelings about a cherry tree in its ephemerally beautiful bloom seemed totally different from the feelings that the average American would muster on looking at a blossoming apple

3

tree. The Japanese closeness to nature, akin to deification, seems to lead to a special Japanese feeling toward death."[3] In America, death is romanticised through violence as depicted in movies, song and literature. Our western culture, by contrast to eastern attitudes, has historically viewed death as the enemy to be subdued and defeated.

The truth is that we are born and we will die. Saying it is not the same as knowing it and accepting the fact that death is real. As Luijpen states: "to be man is to exist."[4] The inability to comprehend one's nonexistence is a paralyzing force. Luijpen further states that "there is only one way possible for man to withdraw from the world, namely by death. But through death he ceases to be man."[5]

The finality of death is difficult to comprehend, to accept or even to imagine. For this reason, there is much concern with life after death. If I have no option but to die, what is there for me after I die? Surely there must be something! Would the pain of separation be less intense if we had some guarantee that something pleasant and desirable awaits us after death occurs? Part of the fear of death could also address itself to the fact that we are accustomed to this world as we know it; since we have learned to live, to love and to cope with everday existences that on that basis alone, we like where we are and have no desire to leave, for here is everything of which we can be sure. This is all there is as far as we know. Anything beyond this is a philosophy, a hope, a dream, a faith or a belief.

For thousands of years, civilizations have dealt with attitudes about death and dying in various ways; but always, the underlying emotion was based on fear of the unknown and a deep-seated reluctance to relinquish the known aspects of life on earth. Certain theoretical approaches have carried over into present day influences on the subject. Stannard refers to the Epic of Gilgamesh, for instance, as a time in history dated around 2000 BC when an after-life was believed to be a totally frightening prospect. During that time the idea of a *post mortem* judgement emerged "in response to the anxieties evident in the Gilgamesh epic concerning the psychic emptiness of death."[6] Whether early beliefs that embraced the concept of death as cessation of self or the later philosophy of Christianity that introduced the idea of Heaven, Hell and Purgatory depending upon the quality of life the deceased had lived, the basic fear of death is intermingled within the popular question of life after death. For many people the hope for life after life is a tenacious hope in the struggle to accept their mortality.

People who participate in thanatology sensitivity exercises, when asked to imagine themselves being dead, often state, "I don't feel anything." This does not necessarily mean that they are deliberately avoiding their feelings, but it does suggest that to imagine one's self as a total void is difficult if not impossible. Dr. Elisabeth Kubler-Ross writes that to think of one's own death is a fearful task because "in our unconscious, death is never possible in regard to ourselves. It is inconceivable for our unconscious to imagine an actual ending of our own life here on earth."[7]

The suggestion that death creates a nothingness or psychic emptiness where once there was life is too threatening to consider, and it causes discomfort in many people. Change is a condition which frequently presents a threat to people, sometimes to the point of being intolerable, and death is change of the highest order. Ordinary changes in the lives of people can prompt anxieties and unanswerable questions. The fewer the answers the greater the fear associated with such changes become. It is not unreasonable that people are afraid of death since, if given the choice, most of us would opt for the *status quo*. Maslow describes the phenomenon of catastrophic conflict as being a "pure threat with no alternative or possibilities of choice."[8] We tend to think of death within this context. Still, the inevitableness of death does provide us one choice. As Victor Frankl postulates, when "all the familiar goals in life are snatched away, what remains is the ability to choose one's attitude in a given set of circumstances."[9]

Death is a significant factor in everyone's life. It is now, as throughout history, an area of the greatest human concern, a subject which provokes many feelings and questions and yet provides few satisfactory answers. This is due in part to our learned behavior within a death-denying society. This is not to suggest that fear of death is not an honest emotion; it is rather to emphasize that introspection of one's life is one way of working to become more comfortable with the subject of death. Three important aspects of life are work, love and play. They together comprise the fundamental principles of the good life. When these primary aspects of life are threatened by death, the results are devastating.

> *It is the custom of the Chinese to keep their coffins in their houses where they can be often seen. The ancient Egyptians, at all their feasts, served their guests with some part of a skeleton to put them in mind of their mortality. And, on the day of this coronation, one of the emperors of Constantinople, among other gifts of great value, received the present of a gravestone, to remind him of the coming day when the crown would be taken from his head. And, in the midst of life and health, it would be good for us if we would often think of that hour that will finish our discipline and fix our destiny.*[10]

> *(Public Speakers Library, Leaves of Gold)*

THE ROLE OF RELIGION

The power of the religious influence that shapes our lives determines certain attitudes and actions when we are confronted with death, whether it is our own or the death of someone else.

The most ancient and traditional dispositions for dealing with death and dying were, and are, firmly based on the concepts and values of religious systems. History confirms that the principles of immortality are clearly supported by religious precepts. History supports this assertion by taking us back into prehistoric times and the lives of primitive peoples.

For centuries human beings have pondered death and dying, burial and the concept of rebirth. This need to reconcile the constant realities of death are based on the inability to perceive oneself in the absence of life and the state of being. Stannard supports this thinking by quoting Freud, who wrote "it is indeed impossible to imagine our own death. And whenever we attempt to do so we can perceive that we are in fact still present as spectators. Hence at the bottom no one believes in his own death, or, to put the same thing in another way, in the unconscious, every one of us is convinced of his

6

own immortality."[11] Stannard further postulates that this thinking was not unique to Freud, that others before him also shared this belief. Today there is still no resolution of this age-old concern with death and its meaning to us as individuals. Stannard refers to this need as a dilemma which we, as humans, are "driven to resolve."[12] The inability to resolve the issue presents a disturbing conflict and, writes Stannard, "it is this fundamental dilemma imposed by the existence of death, and the limited knowledge that men necessarily have of it, that Malinowski and other early anthropologists saw as the primary source of religion."[13]

Within every known civilization there have existed certain religious practices by which attitudes toward death and dying were determined and sustained. Certain peoples who inhabited the earth over 500,000 years ago, for example the *Pithecanthropus*, predecessors of Neanderthal man, left no evidence for anthropologists and historians to unravel. This in no way suggests that they were exceptions to religious practices, but only that this part of their history was lost and could not be determined.

It has been established that the Neanderthals, who existed between 100,000 and 25,000 years ago, vigorously participated in religious ceremonies including the generous use of flowers to bury their dead. This practice was a result of their fundamental urgings to show respect and recognition for the dead who had once lived among them and been a part of their lives. However primitive, their culture was based on the premise that human life is a thing of value. They believed, as have most cultures who followed them, that life and death exist on a continuum of natural events and that when death occurs the dead deserves to be respected, acknowledged and appropriately prepared for the next journey. Not only did Neanderthals perform rituals for their dead, they buried them with food and flint utensils to sustain and light their paths, believing that the dead would live on in some inexplicable way.

During the Old Stone Age, between 25,000 and 10,000 years ago, religion was a central theme throughout human cultural activities; whether ceremoniously practiced to assure a successful hunt for food or to assure that the dead would live again, men symbolically provided "blood of life" by painting the bodies of their dead with red paint, "the red tint probably suggesting the color of life."[14] These and other rituals were directed by an important central figure, called a shaman, whose function it was to provide multiple human services for the tribes. Their religious rites and attitudes toward the dead are documented through paintings on the walls of caves in Northern, Southern and Central Spain, and serve as evidence that their religious beliefs strongly influenced their total way of life.

As the Old Stone Age evolved into what is known as the New Stone Age, between 10,000 and 3,000 B.C., these prehistoric people developed more creative skills. They made axes to work with, houses to live in and boats which would introduce them to a totally new way of life. According to Hilliard, they even began "to practice a crude kind of surgery."[15] But aside from these important prehistoric advancements, their religious beliefs were evidenced in the way they handled the burial of their dead. Hilliard writes, "Their funeral ceremonies were still more elaborate: sometimes wives and servants were sacrificed with a dead chief or king - presumably so that he could continue to receive their services in another existence."[16] Many of these primitive religious-based practices have evolved through the years, but in areas yet untouched by modern civilization these ancient rituals are still evident.

In concept and practice in many cultures today, it would seem difficult to distinguish religion from magic since they frequently appear to be synonymous. Hilliard writes that in isolated areas of the world certain cultures "have probably retained some of the characteristics of the real primitives and their religious beliefs and practices may tell us a little more about the religion of primitive man."[17] The quality of magic in "primitive" religious practices can be found in the "the conviction that certain places, persons, things, rituals and events are sacred - to be approached or handled with care, fear and reverence."[18] These sacred substances are sources of great power and in order "to harness this awesome power in his service, the primitive uses a variety of magical procedures. He makes use of 'fetishes' - objects which possess power such as pebbles, bones, and sticks of unusual kind. Or he may call in the aid of the 'shaman',"[19] or witch doctor to assure desired results. It is believed among some cultures today, for example, that not only does a soul dwell in every human but in other creations of nature as well. Some religious beliefs embrace the teachings that souls in search of new homes establish themselves within mountains, hills, streams, trees, stones, rock formations and certain animals. Based on these beliefs, the dead are treated with painstaking reverence and inanimate objects or non-human inhabitants of the earth become awesome and powerful forces to be feared and worshipped. The anticipated reward for such fervent behavior is protection from negative forces and the attraction of personal and group favor and fortune.

History further reveals that civilizations have always lived in environments filled with highly dangerous, life-threatening situations. From prehistoric times to the present era, fear has plagued human existence. It is logical to consider the possibility that the need for basic security and fear of death could indeed be the true basis for religious worship which has evolved over thousands of years into the firmly established aspect of life that it is today.

It is certain that the Egyptians had strong religious belief in life after death and that they worshipped many gods. The Young King Tut (Tutenkamon) is credited with having reversed the proclamation of the *Pharoah* who preceeded him (Amenhotep IV 1379-1361) who advocated the worship of a single god, to assure that the practice of multi-god worship would continue. Hilliard writes that "Under Pharoah Amenhotep IV (1379-1361) Egyptian religion came very near to abandoning the worship of all gods except one."[20] This practice flourished for a time, but changed when the celebrated King Tutenkamon finally succeeded to the throne and "allowed the older forms of worship to revive and Egyptians returned to a worship of many gods."[21]

Religious beliefs in Egypt also embraced the expectations that its rulers and persons of nobility were immortal. In addition to the practice of burying the noble dead with vast amounts of wealth and food, they used incredible skills to embalm and mummify their dead because they believed the soul would return to the body. Inscriptions written on walls and other elaborate preparations were made to assure that the dead would be prepared for the ultimate reunion. Perusal of the renowned "Book Of The Dead" which the Egyptians placed in coffins as a guide for the dead is sufficiently convincing of the seriousness with which they practiced their religious beliefs. This ancient treatise was designed to explain how the soul is judged and to prepare the dead for immortality. All Egyptians did not mummify their dead, but they all made some attempts to preserve the bodies as they believed without exception in life after death through the existence of a divine power.

The Greeks later made a distinctive contribution to European religions by introducing the concept of rational thinking, an occurrance which significantly modified religious practices and manners of worship. The long-range result was an effort to reconcile reason, emotion and will as a more enlightened approach to religion. "The word 'religion' has in fact been given to us by the Romans. It comes from a Latin root meaning to bind fast in mutual obligation and denoted an essential business-like, legal attitude to religion."[22]

In Roman terms it suggested an unemotional, stoic, business-like attitude. Still, during the Roman era funeral rites were elaborately conducted. They practiced cremation and burial but claimed not to believe in life after death. They believed that the spirits dwelled "in a pit below the center point of the city. Three times a year priests raised the stone slab which marked the intersection of the two main streets of the city and released these spirits to return to mingle for a time with the living."[23]

The Hindu religion teaches its followers that there is no death; there is merely transition. To the Hindu death is viewed as a release from one life and the beginning of the next. The faith had its origin in India, but vast numbers of followers are found in Thailand, Ceylon, South Africa and various other parts of the world. At the time of death and during the transition period, bodies are burned on funeral pyres and the ashes are scattered into a holy river. "The status of the funeral Priest is lowest of all (other Priests) since his work involves his becoming polluted through contact with the dead,"[24] Hilliard writes. These rites are conducted with chanting, the wailing of hymns and the haunting sounds blown from conch shells.

"It is the hope of every pious Hindu that after death, his body may be cremated on the banks of the sacred river and his ashes cast upon her waters."[25]

Religion is a matter of cultural learning and a matter of human choice. There are contrasts as well as similarities between all religions. Fiefel says that "the world's major religions have encouraged different attitudes toward death. Although some early Christian martyrs died fearlessly, in eager anticipation of eternal bliss, Christianity has on the whole used its vast influence to make men dread death."[26] This dread is based on the fear of judgment. To be judged is frightening because it connotes goodness and badness, successes and failures, strengths and weaknesses, and when man cannot measure up the judgment becomes awesome. It is overwhelming for many people to be judged by a civil judge, and the prospect of standing before a supreme being to face judgment is terrifying. So it was as Stannard states, "with the Ancient Egyptians, who imagined an awesome face-to-face judgment following their death, and who thus composed long prayers denying culpability in sin and put to use all the artistic and literary powers at their command to ward off an unfavorable verdict."[27] Early Christianity embraced this attitude centuries later.

By contrast the Buddhist religion emphasizes transition without judgment. As Kapleau offers in his analogy, the "flame passing from lamp to candle indicates that rebirth is the continuation of process rather than the transfer of a substance."[28]

However Confucianism, Hinduism, Buddhism, Shintoism or any other religions differ from the Christian views, most of them embrace the concept of the immortality of the human spirit. The Moslems believe with deep conviction that each person's death is preordained and that there will be a resurrection, and their burial rites are conducted with simplicity, dignity and prayer.

Jewish attitudes towards the terminally ill and death and dying are bound by tradition, laws and customs that are centuries old. Jewish beliefs toward life and death are spelled out, as Rabbi Maurice Lamm explains, through "thousands of years of rich tradition which provides us with direction during these moments of crisis. The accumulated wisdom of the ages is a source of great consolation."[29]

Throughout history various peoples have regarded death as a continuation of life. In most cultures these basic attitudes and beliefs were so strong that elaborate preparations and rituals were engaged in to enhance the transitions and journeys from one life into the next.

11

Hicks points out that "our prehistoric ancestors assumed that in some sense and in some form humans continue to exist after their deaths, so as to have a use for the precious objects which were buried with them."[30] But Americans have never embraced these concepts with the same optimistic convictions that other cultures have. On the whole our culture sees death as an extremely frightening and hateful experience, a negative aspect of life to be avoided and denied at all costs. It is within this context that Hick so eloquently asserts that "in his relation to death man is unique among the animal species, and indeed doubly unique. For alone among the animals he knows that he is going to die; and further, he not only knows it but - in an important sense - does not believe it!"[31]

When these well-established defenses are confronted and challenged by the reality of a diagnosis of terminal illness, families and friends are presented with a very unpleasant, almost embarrassing situation that few are equipped to cope with on an open and honest emotional level. Such negative feelings and reactions account for the isolation of dying patients; the lack of support for them and their families; and the absence of a genuine willingness to deal with their real needs. Our society seems to have stronger hope than absolute convictions in the theory of an after life. Evidence of this is the fact that one of the most frequently asked questions in thanatology classes is "do you believe in life after death?" Even when positive responses are offered, they seem not to provide long-lasting comfort to the inquirer. The need to believe appears to be the motivating factor.

Because we are, throughout our history, a death-fearing, death-denying society, we are both emotionally and intellectually programmed not to embrace death without reluctance, emotional struggle and measurable fear. It is not our intention to suggest that we should, only to indicate that we have made significant progress in terms of confronting our own emotions and attitudes about a traditionally terrifying subject. Within the context of learning to cope with death and dying and helping people who are in the process of confronting death, it is despite our old established taboos and negative attitudes that we are finally beginning a renaissance in health care of the most compassionate kind. The sturdy thread of hope that is firmly anchored in the total life of a person tends to penetrate deeper when death threatens the person or one of his own. In the face of death through terminal illness, hope grows stronger and helps to sustain the patient throughout the illness. When death can no longer be denied, when fear of death and hope for recovery are replaced with an attitude of peaceful acceptance and hope for a continuation of life, Curran states that "to be able to say 'we shall overcome' in the face of death is to chant a religious cry."[32] He supports the belief that "only the man of religious values seems able to see death in this kind of victorious light."[33] When death comes, life as we know it will no longer exist. But the hope generated from the acceptance of this finality indicates a continuity of some form of eternal life, just as certain religions teach that life after death will be a new life. Hans Kung states that "even to speak of life 'after' death is misleading: eternity is not characterized by 'before' and 'after'. It means a new life which escapes the dimensions of space and time, a life within God's invisible, imperishable, incomprehensible domain."[34] A person who is dying can find acceptance of his death when he knows that much of his creativity, or his teachings, or his values are preserved through the extension of himself through his children. For example in some cultures and some families the male child is highly prized for these reasons. The male child not only perpetuates the genetic characteristics of his family, he also immortalizes the name.

Religion within the family establishes the values and orientation an individual has towards his fellow humans. He learns to view others in the context set by religious teachings that establish behavior in all settings.

To be effective religion needs to be understood in terms of the role it plays in the circumstances of everyday living. Some individuals' entire lives revolve around their religion. In facing death and dying religion makes sense out of chaos, tragedy, and despair. It is a sustaining force when all other supports or beliefs seem inadequate; it is difficult for humans to let go, to accept the finality that life as we know it ceases to be.

In almost every culture religion is and has been the dominant force in shaping the attitudes of human beings toward the vast experiences associated with living and dying. Throughout history mankind has experimented with various methods of dealing with the omnipresent stresses of living and the challenges of coping with death. The result has been the discovery that in troubled times there are anchors that hold and anchors that sway. History supports the generally believed position that when all else proves to be inadequate, religion is for most people the anchor that holds.

Broom and Selznick say that religion helps make the world around us more acceptable in several basic ways; specifically, "by providing religious rewards and consolations to offset secular failures and personal tragedy, religion facilitates the continuous adaptation of the individual to the circumstances of his life."[35]

The "new life" that Kung speaks of is perhaps made clearer by Gibran who so eloquently offers that:

"Only when you drink from the river of silence shall you
    indeed sing.
And when you have reached the mountain top, then you
    shall begin to climb.
And when the earth shall claim your limbs, then shall
    you truly dance."[36]

The many concepts of death or eternal life are as varied as individual religious teachings and cultures. Still, despite the differences and similarities in our religious orientation toward living and dying, there is a common thread that binds us without exception. As Gibran writes:

"Who can separate his faith from his actions,
or his belief from his occupations?
Who can spread his hours before him,
saying, 'This for God and this for myself,
This for my soul, and this other for my body?'
All our hours are wings that beat
through space from self to self."[37]

MYTHS

"We are afraid of truth, afraid of fortune, afraid of death and afraid of each other."[38]

— *Emerson*

Study Questions: *A PRE-TEST*

Indicate whether the following statements are true or false.

1. Terminal cancer patients, without exception, experience excruciating pain, especially at the time of death.　　　T___F___

2. Terminal patients have no desire to discuss their situation with others. They prefer to be left alone except for assistance with physical comfort.　　　T___F___

3. Terminal patients are so preocupied with their situation that they are interested only in conversation that is related to what is happening to them.　　　T___F___

4. It is emotionally harmful for terminal patients to see indications of sadness in staff members who work closely with them.　　T___F___

5. The family should be discouraged by staff from allowing emotions to show in the presence of terminal patients.　　　T___F___

6. It is highly unprofessional for staff to show emotion.　　　T___F___

7. Terminal patients should be discouraged from expressing themselves in emotional ways.　　　T___F___

8. It is only acceptable for patients to cry if they are women. Men should be strongly discouraged by staff and family from resorting to tears to express their feelings because it is unmanly, a sign of weakness.　　T___F___

Discussion Questions

1. Most people want to live. Does that mean that it is impossible to experience acceptance of death?
2. Do you feel that patients who have family support have no need of supportive intervention from staff?
3. Do you believe that all terminal patients seek religious counseling before they die, whether they are religious, atheistic or agnostic?
4. Are most patients, when informed that their illness is terminal, likely to give up all hope and lose the will to live?
5. Do you believe that most patients would prefer not to be informed of their terminal conditions?
6. Would you prefer not to be told if you had a terminal disease? Explain.

There are as many myths and misconceptions associated with terminal patients as there are people who fear death. Attitudes about death and toward people who are dying need be neither logical or rational. They need only to become indelible in people's minds in order to influence their perception and behavior towards others. Myths that generate negative aspects of human behavior tend to perpetuate and reinforce themselves according to the purposes they serve. For instance, if you believe the following commonly accepted myth, how do you think it might effect your attitude in a real life situation? "Terminal patients who are quiet, uncomplaining and seek no help from others are at peace with themselves; otherwise they would ask for help. They should be left alone except for medical reasons, since to approach them about their feelings would only upset them."

Obviously, to believe that quiet denotes peace could justify avoidance, turning your attention elsewhere. It could cause you to be less alert, therefore less responsive to a withdrawn terminal patient who might, in fact, be in great need of emotional support. The difference between myth and reality and how we respond to the needs of people who are dying lies within our well-developed beliefs about terminal illness and attitudes about death.

The study of death and dying helps us to dispel certain myths that can effect our attitudes and interfere with the practice of good physical and emotional care for terminal patients. The myth of Lazarus for example is among the early known fallacies associated with death and dying. During the fourteenth and fifteenth centuries it was commonly believed that the moment of death was synonymous with excruciating mortal torment. Stannard cites the belief of the Middle Ages that "following his resurrection, Lazarus lived in constant torment with the knowledge that he would have to endure the physical act of dying a second time."[39] During that time in history, various plagues, famines and horrors of wars presented scenes of great human devastation and destruction. Those historical events of human suffering contributed to the development of new myths and perpetuation of old tales and attitudes about death. They have significantly influenced our current beliefs about the subject in many ways. Myths about terminal patients are closely associated with our attitudes about disease itself. Modern misconceptions about cancer are not too different from our image of the plagues that tormented the people of Europe centuries ago.

In America today cancer is the "monster" that heads the list of the most feared catastrophic diseases. Few families in our society remain untouched by its frightful occurrences in one way or another, however remote the connection might be. The very word, cancer, is sufficient to provoke negative feelings and anxiety in people. Cancer is the word most frequently associated with the word terminal. Therefore, before we discuss further some of the myths associated with terminal cancer patients, perhaps we should first examine certain fallacies about the disease itself.

We might begin with word association: Terminal......cancer. The response is immediate and predictable. The feeling is one of anxiety, fear and repulsion. You will find that we do not react the same way or experience the same visceral changes when confronted with the words: emphysema; amyotrophic lateral sclerosis; multiple sclerosis; leukemia; Hodgekin's Disease; or Huntington's Chorea. You may not be familiar with all of these diseases, but you will find that attitudes towards patients afflicted with these lethal disorders tend to be different.

17

There is less tendency to avoid the patients and less tendency to withdraw from or socially isolate patients with these diseases than there is with patients who have cancer. Why do you think there is less fear, less stigma and less panic associated with these catastrophic diseases than there is with a diagnosis of cancer? Why is cancer so terrifying? Why do symptoms that might indicate the presence of cancer cause such emotional trauma? And why does cancer cause such emotional trauma? And why does cancer, diagnosed, send the patient and the family into immediate emotional tailspins? Since the answers appear to be obvious these questions might seem totally ridiculous. But are they? Given more deliberate consideration, you will discover that there is a universal and paralyzing psychological fear of cancer that generates strong negative attitudes not only towards the disease but also towards patients who suffer from it. Part of the reason is that cancer causes death. But so do the other diseases mentioned here. Is death the only basis for our great fear of cancer? It is certainly a justifiable thought. But we believe there is more, and in support of this position we hypothesize that the reasons are inexorably connected with the following prevailing myths about cancer:

MYTH #1. CANCER IS AN INSIDIOUS DISEASE THAT EATS PEOPLE ALIVE.

The average person who has seen the physical damage and disfigurement that can result from cancer of the face and throat might be inclined to question whether the above statement is a myth. Such a question would be understandable, since in severe cases it is not uncommon to see the absence of a nose or other sections missing from the face or throat. This is admittedly a most unpleasant sight to witness. Such mutilations, however, are the results of surgical procedures and are not caused, as many people believe, by cancer "eating away" at the patient's flesh. This visual evidence of cancerous destruction tends to strengthen belief in one of the popular myths among non-medical people, professionals and laymen alike. It follows, therefore, that this common misconception creates terror in the minds of people regarding what goes on inside the body of a patient who has cancer. At a more basic level is the very frightening thought of "what if I get it?" It is, after all, totally intolerable to perceive oneself being "eaten alive." This fearful image is compounded by the fact that cancer inside the body is beyond the

18

range of normal vision. What is happening inside the body cannot be observed and the tormenting imaginings of being devoured by a disease which "eats from the inside" and "rots the body" provide the only perceptions of what is happening within a person's body. It is understandable that cancer in this sense is perceived as a horror beyond description, a fearful and hateful thing.

THE TRUTH IS: CANCER DOES NOT "EAT AWAY" AT INTERNAL ORGANS.

Cancer is a catastrophic disease that destroys the body by producing abnormal cells in great abundance. "Cancer becomes a destructive process when a small group of cells ceases to live in harmony and begins to invade and destroy neighboring groups of cells."[40] These irregular cells become widespread and aggressive. Characteristically cancer increases in size and forces normal cells and tissues aside to make accommodations (space) for itself. This maleficent uncontrolled activity of expanding cancer cells is the process of malignancy. The result of this persistent process of cancerous growth forcing space for itself within the body may be that with the progressive increase in the size of the cancer, its bulk may interfere with the function of the involved anatomical site."[41]

This progressive state of malignancy can occur within any organ or any part of the body, whether it is the face, the spleen, the breast, the lung or the brain. The "crowding" effect that occurs inside the head when there is cancer involvement in the brain, for example, is what accounts for the excruciating headaches that many terminal patients experience. Within this context, perhaps it is easier to understand the rationale and the benefits hoped for in the application of radiation and chemotherapy as attempts to "retard the cancer growth", since these efforts, if successful, provide physical relief for the patient even if treatment is insufficient to save the person's life.

MYTH # 2. ALL CANCER PATIENTS SUFFER EXCRUCIATING PAIN.

There is little doubt that fear of pain is a universal truth. But the common belief that cancer and unbearable pain are

19

inherently synonymous is a myth. This common belief contributes to negative, awkward and anxious behavior toward terminal patients. Families frequently speak in tones of disbelief or uncertainty when referring to the cancer patient who "is experiencing no pain" or regarding the relative who dies but who "never had any pain at all." Relatives sometimes wonder if the staff "told them the truth," or if the patient "hid the pain to spare the family worry."

THE TRUTH IS: CANCER AND PAIN ARE NOT INNATELY SYNONYMOUS.

Contrary to popular belief, pain is not an outstanding characteristic of cancer. There are however some exceptions, and bone cancer is one of them. Cancer of the bone can be extremely painful and, in some cases, very difficult to control, but it is not unusual for many patients with cancer to never suffer extraordinary pain. There are many cancer patients who experience no pain at all.

MYTH # 3: CANCER IS CONTAGIOUS

This myth is probably a carry-over from the past when cancer was commonly believed to be a form of syphillis. It is part of the stigma of cancer and many people still have the uneasy feeling that cancer is a contagious disease. It was not too long ago that tuberculosis (which is contagious) was the great stigma among frightful diseases. Patients who suffered T.B. were separated from the main hospital and placed in "pest houses" where they were feared, isolated and scorned. It was a "shameful" disease; embarrassing to patients and families; contagious and incurable. With the advent of effective drug therapy, tuberculosis is no longer so fearful and stigmatized. It can now be arrested, cured and controlled. It no longer carries the threat of certain death for its victims which was once a realistic possibility. Today, cancer ranks highest among our most dread diseases. Cancer is stigmatized as being contagious even in the minds of many people who openly profess to believe otherwise. Because of the high death rate and because it is so feared, people are reluctant to accept reassurance to the contrary. Perhaps it is easy to believe that anything so terrible must be contagious. It might take a scientific breakthrough in combatting the death rate caused by cancer to reverse this subtle and negative attitude toward the disease.

MYTH # 4: A DIAGNOSIS OF CANCER AUTOMATICALLY MEANS DEATH

There are different types of cancer and many forms of cancer are curable. All cancer patients do not die of the disease. Many patients diagnosed as having cancer survive the disease and die of other causes. Within our communities and through mass media, we are frequently made aware of deaths caused by cancer and it is sufficient to convince us that myth number four is unequivocally true. We do not as often hear of the statistics which show the survival rate of patients who have been cured through early diagnosis and treatment, but the numbers are significant.

MYTH # 5: CANCER SMELLS TERRIBLE.

This common myth that cancer "smells terrible" is closely connected in predictable ways to myth number one which states that "cancer eats the body or rots the insides" of people. Perpetuation of this fallacious assumption is probably caused by various experiences of people who encounter unpleasant odors, personal conditions and circumstances of terminal patients during untimely hospital nursing facility or home visits. This myth is also most likely based to some extent on the experiences associated with patients who suffer cancer of the face and throat. People who have seen these conditions and noticed the unpleasant odors would naturally make such an assumption which is logical, but invalid. The unpleasant odors associated with cancer of the face and throat are due to the inability to sterilize the mouth and the boney areas of the face, and to the lack of control of the mucous drainage from the sinus and throat. Occasionally, cancer of the breast might produce unpleasant smells but this situation usually develops only in very advanced cases.

Cancer of the prostate produced bad odors twenty or thirty years ago, but such conditions were due to the methods of surgery used which made healing very difficult. The old surgical method known as *super pubic prostatectomy,* for example, has been eliminated by more modern surgical techniques known as *trans urethral resection* (TUR); this procedure, together with chemical treatment, has eliminated the problem of offensive odor which also contributed to perpetuating myth number five.

Before the advent of modern medicine, many patients did smell bad. That was because old surgical wounds did not

21

heal properly and sometimes did not heal at all. In the era before the French scientist, Louis Pasteur, devised the revolutionary process of sterilization, scores of patients died due to dirty conditions; unwashed hands passing germs from one patient to another, and from lethal infections due to contaminated surgical instruments and general unsterilized conditions. During that early period in history, people were, in fact, better off at home where their families could give them personal attention in more sanitary surroundings than as patients confined to hospitals which operated under substandard conditions.

It was, in fact, such disdainful circumstances as these that gave foundation to the long-lasting public attitude that hospitals were places "where people go to die." Physical conditions in hospitals during that time frequently presented shocking scenes of human deprivation and suffering. This combination of unfortunate situations throughout history accounts for many of the myths that persist today regarding the nature of certain kinds of disease and the fate of terminal patients. Myths that are generally accepted as truth about terminal patients are of significance, since they all too frequently lead to the self-fulfilling prophecy that "nothing can be done to really help someone who is dying." Such myths inevitably encourage the tendency to avoid, to isolate and to abandon patients at the very time when the need is greatest for close human contact, interaction and emotional support.

Care and treatment of terminal patients has not been fully examined in our society because the topic of death has been taboo for so long. Myths about catastrophic diseases, therefore, have not been considered for their negative effects on patient care for the same reasons. Now that death and dying as a topic of discussion is finally out of the closet, we are challenged to seek ways to overcome obsolete theories and negative attitudes in terminal care. This effort requires a closer look at what we have long believed about terminal patients. Our present attitudes will be affected by our old perceptions and will determine how well the needs of dying patients are met.

SUMMARY
Statements 1 through 8 on the Pre-Test are all false. Each of the items will be discussed at various points in the book to help you better understand why the statements are

untrue and how they interfere with good patient care in actual practice situations. Myths about terminal patients and about catastrophic disease, cancer in particular, are interrelated and tend to reinforce themselves because they justify our reluctance to become therapeutically involved with people who are dying.

Myths are self-serving in the sense that they strengthen old prejudices and delay the process of change in learning to modify attitudes toward a difficult subject such as death and dying. Quiet patients sometimes need our help the most. They are the patients who challenge our ability to perceive their unspoken needs. Some patients are quiet because they are trying to be "good patients," not wanting to cause any problems for the staff; or they might be terrified and unable to call attention to their needs by verbalizing their problems. Terminal patients often reflect the attitudes of their families, who are also experiencing the stress and confusion of trying to cope. Non-assertive people are frequently non-assertive patients. Few people have learned how to "be sick." Many patients are victims of terminal illness who have never before experienced a serious illness of any kind. They have no way of knowing what to expect from others or what is expected of them by others. It is therefore necessary for staff to reach out to patients and offer support to families. Health care providers are expected to become more aware of the unique needs of terminal patients as well as the needs of families. In order to do this, caretakers are challenged to learn more about the special ways of helping dying patients through therapeutic methods. Dispelling crippling myths that limit our capacities is one step in the right direction.

The discussion questions and the study questions in the Pre-Test at the beginning of this section can be used for further exploration to enhance learning in group discussions. They are specifically designed to help you determine the depth of your own understanding of the nature of cancer in relation to death. A major step in this direction will be taken as you learn to question your own well-established attitudes toward death and dying, and to develop the willingness to rid yourself of certain misconceptions and of ingrained myths that are counter-productive to the therapeutic process of effective terminal care.

REFERENCES

* A quote by Linda Dold Robinson "Gerontological Nursing Research," *Nursing and the Aged*, edited by Irene Mortenson Burnside, McGraw Hill Book Company, 1976, p. 586.
1. Bryant, William Cullen, "Thanatopsis."
2. Peck, Rosalie, *THRESHOLD* (unpublished).
3. Shneidman, *Deaths of Man*, Quadrangle, The New York Times Book Co., 1973.
4. Luijpen, William A., Ph.D., *Existential Phenomenology*, Duquesne University Press, Pittsburgh, PA.
5. Luijpen, William A., Ph.D., *Existential Phenomenology*, Duquesne University Press, Pittsburgh, PA.
6. Stannard, David E., *The Puritan Way of Death: A Study In Religion, Culture and Social Change*, Oxford University Press, New York, 1977.
7. Kubler-Ross, Elisabeth, M.D., Ph.D., *On Death and Dying*, MacMillan, New York, 1969.
8. Maslow, Abraham H., *Motivation and Personality*; Second Edition, Harper & Row, Publishers, New York, Evanston and London.
9. Frankl, Viktor, M.D., Ph.D., *Man's Search For Meaning*, Beacon Press, Boston, 1969.
10. Public Speakers Library, *Leaves of Gold*, Coslett Publishing Co., Williamsport, PA.
11. Stannard, David E., *The Puritan Way of Death: A Study In Religion and Social Change,* Oxford University Press, New York, 1977.
12. Stannard, David E., *The Puritan Way of Death: A Study In Religion and Social Change,* Oxford University Press, New York, 1977.
13. Stannard, David E., *The Puritan Way of Death: A Study In Religion and Social Change,* Oxford University Press, New York, 1977.
14. Stannard, David E., *The Puritan Way of Death: A Study In Religion and Social Change,* Oxford University Press, New York, 1977.
15. Hilliard, Frederick H., *How Men Worship*, Roy Publishers, Inc., New York, 1965.
16. Hilliard, Frederick H., *How Men Worship*, Roy Publishers, Inc., New York, 1965.

17. Hilliard, Frederick H., *How Men Worship*, Roy Publishers, Inc., New York, 1965.
18. Hilliard, Frederick H., *How Men Worship*, Roy Publishers, Inc., New York, 1965.
19. Hilliard, Frederick H., *How Men Worship*, Roy Publishers, Inc., New York, 1965.
20. Hilliard, Frederick H., *How Men Worship*, Roy Publishers, Inc., New York, 1965.
21. Hilliard, Frederick H., *How Men Worship*, Roy Publishers, Inc., New York, 1965.
22. Hilliard, Frederick H., *How Men Worship*, Roy Publishers, Inc., New York, 1965.
23. Hilliard, Frederick H., *How Men Worship*, Roy Publishers, Inc., New York, 1965.
24. Hilliard, Frederick H., *How Men Worship*, Roy Publishers, Inc., New York, 1965.
25. Hilliard, Frederick H., *How Men Worship*, Roy Publishers, Inc., New York, 1965.
26. Fiefel, Herman, *The Meaning of Death*, McGraw-Hill, New York, 1959.
27. Stannard, David E., *The Puritan Way of Death: A Study In Religion, Culture and Social Change*, Oxford University Press, New York, 1977.
28. Kapleau, Philip (editor) *The Wheel of Death*, assisted by Patterson, Simon, A collection of writings from Zen Buddhists and others on Death, Rebirth, Dying, Harper & Row Publishers, New York, Evanston, San Francisco, London, 1971, p. xiii.
29. Lamm, Maurice, Rabbi, *The Jewish Way In Death and Mourning*, Jonathan David Publishers, New York, 1969.
30. Hick, John H., *Death and Eternal Life*, Harper & Row Publishers, New York, Hagerstown, San Francisco, London, 1976.
31. Hick, John H., *Death and Eternal Life*, Harper & Row Publishers, New York, Hagerstown, San Francisco, London, 1976.
32. Curran, Charles A., *Religious Values, In Counseling and Psychotherapy*, 1969.
33. Curran, Charles A., *Religious Values, In Counseling and Psychotherapy*, 1969.
34. Kung, Hans, *On Becoming A Christian*, Doubleday & Company, Inc., Garden City, New York, 1976.

35. Broom, Leonard, and Selznick, Philip, *Sociology*, Third Edition, Harper & Row, Publishers, New York, 1963.
36. Gibran Kahlil, *The Prophet*, Alfred A. Knopf, New York, 1926, Thirteenth Printing, 1969.
37. Gibran, Kahlil, *The Prophet*, Alfred A. Knopf, New York, 1926. Thirteenth Printing, 1969.
38. Emerson, Ralph Waldo, *Selected Prose and Poetry*, Holt, Rinehart and Winston, New York. Tenth Printing, 1961.
39. Stannard, David E., *The Puritan Way of Death: A Study In Religion, Culture and Social Change*, Oxford University Press, New York, 1977.
40. American Cancer Society, Inc., *A Cancer Service Book For Nurses*.
41. American Cancer Society, Inc., *A Cancer Source Book For Nurses*.

PART II

CARE AND TREATMENT
OF TERMINAL PATIENTS

SIGNIFICANCE OF ATTITUDES TOWARD TERMINAL PATIENTS

Among the most significant health care needs in our society is the need for change in our attitudes toward terminal patients. It is a common assumption that people who work in health care institutions with dying patients are automatically prepared to help terminal patients to wrestle with, sort out and work through their feelings about death and dying. It is too frequently true that staff members are themselves emotionally incapable of offering sustaining comfort to the terminal patient due to their own unresolved fears and feeling about their own mortality. As Leonard Pearson states, "despite the universality of death, the subject has long been viewed as a taboo area, especially by the professionals in the health field who are closest to it - physicians, nurses, social workers, and others."[1]

In order for most people to continue their work with terminal patients from day to day, it is necessary for them to develop their own individual patterns of coping with their emotions and, too often, these feelings of discomfort are not shared with other staff. This effort to cope and function in solitary fashion contributes to the formation of a certain distance between patient and practitioner. "Mr. A. just stopped breathing," is the way one nurse informed the doctor that a patient had just died. She looked very sad and her voice was flat as she explained to a staff member that she "heard" what she had just said to the doctor and that she was worried about the "casual" way in which she had begun to accept the deaths of her patients. She was an excellent nurse and a caring person, but the frequency of deaths on her service was wearing on her nerves. She realized the "too casual" sound of her words, but she needed to tell someone that she didn't feel that way at all. The doctor understood her feelings, for he felt the same way.

Mervyn poses the question "What contributes to this type of nursing care and treatment of the hospitalized dying patient? First we live in a society which focuses on youth and a dying patient is a reminder that youth and life are not to last forever. How many nurses or doctors can be comfortable in the presence of someone whose dying forecasts their own future?"[2] Many people, whether professional or not, are not accustomed to sharing their innermost feelings with other people; so what do they do with them? They suppress them

29

day after day and continue to work under stress. But such feelings do emerge from time to time and build into attitudes that protect caretakers from becoming involved with patients who are dying and in need of the emotional support that they are unable to provide. The answer to this problem lies in educational opportunities for caretakers. Since most people are afraid of death and the subject of death, it is through education that people will learn to express how they feel about the death of others as well as about their own death. This new trend in our society is evidenced through increasing numbers of graduate school programs, various workshops and seminars designed for professional and ancillary personnel to learn to work with individuals who are dying and to gain insight into their own concept of death.

Everyone who works around a terminally ill patient should be responsible and prepared to provide comfort, whether they are doctors or housekeepers. Everyone needs to be ready because it is unpredictable when and to whom a patient will reach out for comfort. Most patients initiate talk about dying, but most caretakers are not emotionally prepared to respond appropriately. It is necessary to uproot and disperse the myths and traditional training which have for years dictated sterotyped patterns of behavior for health care professionals that preclude the human element in the care and treatment of terminal patients. The old dictums against "getting involved" stand in the way of quality patient care. The health care worker, to be effective, must be involved. Travelbee says that the old nursing exhortation about "not getting involved with patients has probably done more harm over a longer period of time to more people than any other 'nurse-ism' has done or is likely to do."[3] This is indicative also for other health care professionals. It is a risk to become involved, vulnerable to pain and rejection. The dying person will leave us and part of us will die with him. We shy away because once we become involved, our lives become irrevocably changed. The goal of health care workers is to develop a human to human relationship in which empathy occurs. Travelbee describes empathy as a condition in which "one shares in the psychological state of another but not to the extent of thinking and feeling as the other person. To empathize is to 'share' in but to stand apart from the object of one's empathy." She further states: "through an empathetic

30

moment a bond is formed with another and a closeness develops without being submerged by the involvement."[4]

Patients are extemely sensitive to the attitudes of staff. They can sense fear and indifference, and they are able to perceive correctly that rejection might follow. The fear of abandonment is a very real concern of terminal patients. Families, like staff, are sometimes very likely to withdraw from the dying patient because they cannot tolerate the presence of death. Many family members are unable to cope with their feelings and will sometimes stop visiting terminally ill relatives. Others stay outside the room, fearful that they might cry in their presence.

Well-trained staffs are in touch with their own feelings; they are aware of the feelings of their co-workers; they are supportive of each other; they know their emotional limitations; they are capable of handling their own feelings and of relying on support from others. With this combination of strengths, they are not only prepared and capable of supporting their patients, but are also involved in teaching, supporting and enabling survivors to cope effectively during the ordeal of impending death of a relative. A well-trained efficient staff lives and works within a human chain of emotional strength which supports their own needs.

This is not to suggest the idea of a super-staff, but rather an atmosphere in which staff needs are given priority through education that enables staff people to function more comfortably in their assignments to these emotionally draining experiences. Attitudes of staff are based on (1) feelings about the nature of their work; (2) traditional feelings about death and dying that they bring into their work; (3) circumstances and atmosphere associated with their assigned duties; (4) outlets or lack of outlets for ventilation of feelings in relation to their work; and (5) opportunities for change and improvement of job conditions and out-moded regulations.

Most patients want to talk about what is happening to them. They have many questions to ask and many feelings to share. Patients who have had the opportunity to ventilate and who receive support from staff have indicated that having someone to talk to was among the most helpful aspects of their care. The chance to unburden themselves is highly therapeutic even when certain answers cannot be provided. They use the opportunity to unburden themselves

31

to staff who seem to understand their needs and their emotional pain. Health care professionals are frequently struggling with unresolved grief of their own; grief as well as guilt that they have not been able to deal with. Trying to cope with their own feelings becomes too much for many caretakers when they are called upon to offer support to patients who remind them of their own fears and their own emotional problems. It becomes easy to simply avoid the source of such additional burdens. Patients who are already in deep distress are confused by staff members who avoid talking with them. Many patients do not realize the anxiety that the practitioner is experiencing. Certain medical procedures must be followed and staff is held accountable for the provision of these particular services. But patients do notice when, during the process, caretakers avoid eye contact, when services are performed as quickly as possible in order to effect a hasty retreat. "I think she wanted to talk about it, but I didn't know what to say to her," one staff member said. "What did you say?" asked another. "I didn't say anyting, I just left." Or, "I told her not to talk like that." Or, "I tried to change the subject, but she just closed her eyes and then I left."

More than not knowing how to respond to terminal patients, most caretakers are unable to stay, to linger. People who are highly uncomfortable talking with terminal patients can find a million convenient reasons to leave. It is an intolerable feat for many people to talk with a terminal patient for any length of time, no matter what the topic of conversation might be. Dying patients do not want to talk about dying in every conversation they initiate with other people. They have other thoughts and interests and needs, the same as anyone else. But when people are engaged in talking with them it seems very difficult to relate to the patient in an ordinary fashion. "This is not just any person I am talking to. This is a terminal person! A dying person!" Too often, the "awe" they feel comes through and causes stilted, artificial attempts at interaction that are perceived by the patient; it is uncomfortable and embarrassing patient and caretaker alike. In such situations, meaningful dialogue is hardly ever possible and attempts at conversation are short lived and unsatisfying to both parties. As a result, caretakers feel guilty and uneasy and patients feel insignificant and rejected.

On the other hand, patients do not need the opposite attitude too often exemplified in the "blythe spirit" type of death-denying practitioner who breezes into the room full of wit and cheer and behaves in a superficial manner that suggests "all is well." A masquerade of "isn't it a lovely morning," and "how are 'we' today?" is a charade that patients neither need or appreciate. This attitude is displayed by the most frightened staff members. They mean well , but they are not really in touch with their own feelings. They try hard to mask their anxieties in facial and verbal expessions and in tone of voice. They smile too much and frequently inappropriately; and they are the most surprised, confused and hurt when to their bright offering of "and what can I do for you today?" the turned-off patient replies without a trace of emotion, "not a damned thing."

Effective caretakers are aware of their strengths and their weaknessess. They learn and develop their own individual styles of working with terminal patients and co-workers. Staff members are as individual in their ways and manners and personalities as are the patients they serve. But each person must learn his own particular style through education, introspection, practice, trial and error, determination and mutual sharing.

There are basic human prerequisites in working with terminal patients that are no different from working with any other patient. Among these are respect and a sincere desire to be of assistance and to offer emotional comfort. There is within this attitude a willingness to learn. This is the foundation on which all else is based in caring for terminal patients. It does the patient more harm that good to risk sharing deep and painful feelings with caretakers who, out of fear and uncertainty, respond in inappropriate ways. Methods of working with terminal patients in ways that are therapeutic can be learned. There is nothing mysterious or magical in the process. The most difficult task in preparing to help the patient is learning to know ones self in relation to a dying person. Learning to recognize and identify the gut-feelings one feels at the mention of the word - death; at the sight of a terminal patient in varying degrees of deterioration; at the time when one is performing a service or applying a specific procedure; at the moment a patient attempts to engage the caretaker in conversation; at the moment a patient begins to cry. After all, as Dr. Cicely Saunders writes, "our attitude toward the dying patient betrays a good deal of our attitude toward people in general, and of course, of our own interpretation of the meaning of living and dying. So often, it is we who need rehabilitation, not the patient, just as it is the psychology of the seeing rather than the psychology of the blind that is the problem."[5]

If we are to be genuinely concerned for the feelings and attitudes of patients, we must first direct our attention and effort toward tolerance, understanding and change of our own.

EMOTIONAL NEEDS OF THE DYING

In American society, our entire lives are geared toward seeking the good life. We are heavily influenced by the mass media to do certain things or to buy certain products and to have certain experiences in order to gain some kind of mythological happiness and security. As we seek this elusive utopia, we are continally reinforced with the concept that this "good life" is all there is. So when major disruptions such as loss of property, loss of family and loss of health threaten us, we become not only anxious; we come face to face with the reality of our mortality. We tend not to consider that on the continuum of life and death, we are all dying.

Any disruption in life, such as a terminal illness, creates negative feelings. The good life for many people is the attainment of financial security, maintaining good health, and looking forward to old age. To many people, this represents a form of immortality since few people consider the reality of their own death. Many individuals do say "yes, I am going to die," but when faced with the reality of death through terminal illness, the person goes through definite emotional changes. In our society, we have been traditionally programmed to view death as an intrusion on life rather than as an integral part of life. In reality, one cannot be separated from the other since life and death move on a continuum.

We have learned to appreciate the good life but we have not learned to acknowledge the fact that we are mortal. If one learns throughout life that happiness is fleeting, it becomes possible to recognize that we experience small losses continually throughout life; this basically, is nature's way of telling us that life is a process of transition. It is nature's way of helping us to view death not as the enemy, but rather to accept it as the natural, inevitable consequence of living.

Since in America we are just recently becoming able to even discuss death, in order to meet the needs of patients who are dying and families who survive them we must first meet certain needs of our own. Among these is our need to know basic truths in terminal care. What are the needs of the dying patient? Unless common human needs are recognized, the probability of their being met is left to chance. We cannot plan for that which we do not know.

The needs of people who are in the ultimate process of dying can be broadly considered within two major categories: (1) the physiological, and (2) the psychological. Man as a whole must be viewed as a whole. The needs of a dying person therefore must be viewed within this context. All of us have problems with the emotional aspect of death. The physiological needs of terminal patients are more clearly defined and understood than the emotional stresses the dying person experiences. Meeting the emotional as well as the physical needs of patients amounts to closer proximity, in fact and in concept, to treatment of the total patient. in order to move into effective emotional care of a terminal patient, the health care worker must first establish a basic rapport with the person in order to begin to learn how the patient is experiencing his situation. What does it mean to enter a rapport with another? It means simply to discipline your ability to relate to another person in a fashion that is honest, purposeful, and appropriate to the circumstances. it means to finely develop your five senses and to perfect the art of listening. Effective listening is not as simple to achieve as it may sound, for in order to listen with the "third ear," we must first be able to have awareness of our own deep feelings and what is going on inside our own minds and bodies at the same time that the patient is communicating his feelings and his needs to us. Awareness of one's own feelings and the simultaneous awareness of what the patient means by what he is saying is the essence of empathy. It is the sharing in the world of another. It is this development in a human to human relationship that spells the major difference between empathy and sympathy. Empathy, defined psychologically by Zderad, is the "process of subject - object fusion or the subjective state in which the process culminates; it is an ex-

35

periencing of oneness with another. It is a feeling into the other person's thinking and feeling, his psyche, his situation and needs, his private world."[6] This kind of relationship with a dying person affirms his personhood and reinforces whatever ego strengths he has left. This is crucial for the dying patient as he begins to cope with the prospect of his non-being. Le Shan and Le Shan state: "His being is cared for unconditionally, and so he cares for it himself. The presence of the therapist affirms the importance of the here and now."[7]

Two major facets in the patient/practitioner relationship are: that as the patient, his needs are assessed and met by the practitioner. As a client, the person becomes involved in the process of his care. This is the aspect in patient care that is crucial for the practitioner to know: when to do for and when to do with; which will allow the human person to grow from the experience of dying. It is within this relationship that the practitioner also grows. This experience for the practitioner, as with any process of growth, is not without pain. Gibran refers to growth through pain in this way: "Your pain is the breaking of the shell that encloses your understanding. Even as the stone of the fruit must break, that its heart may stand in the sun, so must you know pain."[8]

Dr. Elisabeth Kubler-Ross delineated the process of grief experienced by terminal patients in five states observed during her work with dying patients. She identified these transitions as *denial, anger, bargaining, depression,* and *acceptance.*[9] When threatened by catastrophic disease, a person's whole life is thrown into an emotional tailspin which precedes, accompanies and compounds the subsequent process of physical discomfort and deterioration. No one is prepared to find himself in such a position, so a patient will experience a wide range of emotional trauma and change. The practitioner is thus challenged to provide an anchor of emotional stability through therapeutic intervention while the patient fights for life and struggles to maintain self-hood.

Looking at the stages of dying as presented by Dr. Kubler-Ross, we can learn to recognize and appreciate the similarities, the differences and the individuality of terminal patients. No two people react to dying or to death in precisely the same way.

Dr. George Engel described three stages of grief experiences by a relative of a loved one who died as *shock and disbelief, developing awareness,* and finally, *restitution and recovery.*[10] The similarities in behavior of the patient and his survivors become more obvious to the practitioner who becomes aware of their emotional needs during the course of their multi-faceted crisis situation.

When a person learns that he has a fatal illness, *denial* is the cushion that goes into immediate action to assuage the impact of the terrible shock that invariably accompanies such devastating information. "There must be some mistake?" "I can't believe this." All kinds of mechanisms to deny the truth go into action at such a time. Shock numbs the senses. *Denial* allows for unconscious mobilization of the psyche to fight a fierce battle for survival. *Denial* as a first reaction is a healthy defense mechanism against an overwhelming blow. In the subconscious mind, there is lurking the controlled awareness of the possibility that it might be true, but this feeling must remain submerged until the patient is able to gradually become cognizant of it. When this insight begins to form, the patient might begin to signal it to others, but people might not be prepared to either hear or acknowledge it because they are still stuck at the point of their own *denial.* This is a normal reaction, since the patient's own insight into the possibility of truth is still at a level of vagueness and ambiguity, and hope is still very strong. Kubler-Ross describes this: "The one thing that usually persists through all these stages is hope."[11]

As the patient exhausts the first gargantuan wave of denial and perceives that the prognosis might possibly be true, the second stage, *anger,* sets in. It is at such time as these that a patient might curse you, or God. He might chase away a well-meaning person who even suggests that religious counseling could possibly be beneficial. It is at this time that people cry out loud or scream in desparate silence, "Why me?" "What have I done to deserve this?" "Why my child?" "Why my husband," "Why my wife?" "Why?" "Why?" "Why?" When tragedy comes to a person, on a gut-level, they need to find answers to "why not someone else?" "why not anyone else?" A therapist once risked a lot by asking a wife who was nearing hysteria and insisting on an answer to "why me?", "Would you rather it was I?" The wife heard the connection. The short circuit in her brain responded to the gentle tone of the therapist's voice verbalizing a shocking

37

thought. Her response was a look of stunned surprise followed by submission to a deep catharsis. The therapeutic support that she received allowed the risk to strengthen rather than weaken the patient/therapist relationship which was already well established and based on mutual trust and respect. It is not a technique to consider using indiscriminately. The point, however, is that when tragedy strikes, people seek answers from any source. It is very frustrating for people in emotional pain to find that there are no satisfactory answers to "why me?" The question is as old as life itself. People have always wondered why. It is this human need that prompted Kurt Vonnegut to state in Slaughter House Five, "there is no why. Like a moth drawn to an amber flame, the moment simply is."[12]

We must learn to let people rage and to vent deep emotions. Encourage them to express their feelings. Let them know that it is all right to cry and to feel helpless in the face of overwhelming circumstances. Show your respect for their feelings by supporting them. They will perceive your humanness and will not be embarrassed or afraid that you are judging them. Unless people are allowed to find this kind of support, they will experience difficulty moving into the third phase, which is *bargaining*.

People bargain all the time for the things that are important to them. At horse races, bettors bargain with such statements as: "Please let my horse come in and I'll never gamble again as long as I live. Another example might be, "please let me get over this hangover, and I'll never take another drink." Seldom do we make such strong promises unless the stakes are high and the issue is of great importance to us; and to most of us nothing is more important than life. When patients begin to work through the initial bursts of rage, and the haunting thoughts persist that their illness is lethal, they begin to bargain for life. It might take the form of bargaining that "the doctor made a mistake;" that there will be remission;" "that a cure will be found before it is too late;" "that a certain procedure will restore good health;" to "give me one more year to live." In return, the patient might promise everything from going to church every Sunday to dedicating his entire life to the service of God. The promises are fervent and boundless. And the patients mean every word of it. This process is continual until bargaining is no longer a realistic goal to the patient. The signs and symptoms of deterioration begin to register. At this point the patient moves into the fourth stage of terminal illness which Kubler-Ross describes as *depression*.

This phase of *depression* is as normal as any of the other stages. The feeling is very real. The person is beginning to realize that he is going to die. Normal everyday losses can cause deep depression depending upon the importance of the lost object or person. Depression is a significant aspect of loss even when the loss is not caused by death. When the loss of a significant object or person occurs, we grieve accordingly. A person who is dying is in the process of experiencing total loss. To lose everything and everyone, including oneself, imposes a tremendous emotional burden on a terminal patient. The depression is real and unfathomable. The extent of grief is the signal that they are aware of impending death.

This process of grief continues while the patient struggles with the pain of losses which have already occurred: the lifestyle, the independence as a functioning, productive, healthy individual. The person grieves for what he is losing: his family and friends, his accomplishments, material comforts and plans for the future. He also grieves for his self. The essence of being oneself will be relinquished. No loss could be greater than that.

These are very sensitive times for terminal patients. Caretakers need to be aware of the patient's need for therapeutic intervention and to know when intervention becomes intrusion. The best way to determine this is by investing sufficient time in each patient throughout his or her illness in order to perceive their moods and determine their needs. Intervention that is supportive does not always require dialogue. Patients in a truly therapeutic environment sense when others are sufficiently aware of their needs to allow the patient the emotional space that he requires at a given time.

Under these circumstances it is quite appropriate for the practitioner, when in doubt, to ask if the patient needs any help at that moment. In other words, by keeping in touch with your own feelings and your own needs, you will learn to know when to back off. The health care worker must recognize that a simple sense of "thereness" gives to the patient a certain security and comfort, knowing that he is not alone and will not be abandoned. There comes the time when dying patients need less and less dialogue. Their greatest need for emotional support is provided through a staff that remains sensitive to their needs and available to meet them.

Patients who die well have been able to grieve openly and without restraint. They might gradually come to depend more on one particular caretaker, and they may feel more comfortable in the presence of one loved one who can handle the situation in a supportive, serene and understanding way. It will probably be a friend or a member of the family who is able to be comfortable in an atmosphere of understanding mutual silence; someone who makes no demands on the patient in order to find comfort for himself. As the patient moves into the fifth and final stage, which is *acceptance*, he begins to separate himself from all emotional ties. This phenomenon must occur if nature's way of providing a peaceful death is to take place.

The person still feels love for his family and friends, and still wishes a good life for them, but death has become a reality. What is, is; and the patient accepts it. He has now made his closure by letting go. Nature prepares organisms for death the same as it does for birth. The terminal patients who are fortunate enough to be supported throughout their ordeal are able to move into the moment of death in peace.

The final stage in the process of dying is one of peaceful acceptance of the inevitable. Doctors Engel and Kubler-Ross observed dying patients and provided invaluable information to help professional caretakers become aware of the emotional needs of survivors and people who are in the process of dying. Death is not the issue in terminal care as much as the process of dying, which is the true challenge to be dealt with.

Practitioners in health care need not know patients from the onset of their lethal illness in order to be therapeutically involved. Remember, as health care workers we need to "meet the client where he is." Assess the patients needs from the point of his admission to your service. Getting to know the person also means allowing him to know you. Terminal patients hope for a miracle, a cure. They hope that they will not be isolated, neglected and left alone. They hope for help from people who are skilled, empathetic and available. During the course of treatment, terminal patients talk about the same things that any other patients talk about. They are concerned about batting averages, football, politics, inflation, the State of the Union, and if it's winter or summer, what the temperature might be on a given day. During the prolonged span of terminal illness, remember that patients who can are still hoping to recover. They have fantasies of what they are going to do when they "get out of here." For many patients, terminal illness is a very long process. During this time, they are not 100% preoccupied with thoughts of dying. The thread of hope is tremendously strong. Terminal patients relate to the same thoughts that healthy people have. Use this opportunity to discover common points of interest. It could very well range from needlepoint to backgammon. A warm, sincere, friendly approach that is neither jovial nor sad will help you to develop your own style of approaching any patient. These are the basic ingredients crucial to the development of a human to human relationship that is unique between the therapist and the patient who is dying.

THE ULTIMATE ALONENESS OF DYING

The awesomeness of being human is supported by the fact that man essentially is always alone. Man in his aloneness is original He sees similarities between himself and other humans, but basically he is unlike any other. He experiences his situation in his own personal and exceptional way. Paterson and Zderad state that "uniqueness is a universal capacity of the human species. So, 'all-at-once,' while each man is unique; paradoxically, he is also like his fellows. His very uniqueness is a characteristic of his commonality with all other men."[13]

The commonality that exists between the patient and the practitioner is that they share uniquely in the process of dying. The patient experiencing his own death, the practitioner experiencing his involvement in the process in a "thereness:" both grow as a result of the experience. It can be upsetting to a healthy practitioner to witness the gradual deterioration of another human being because it mirrors the caretakers own mortality. This uncomfortable situation can be a profound growth experience for the professional in terminal care, provided that he is able to recognize the fact that the help being provided to the dying person is really an opportunity to share in the process of another person's dying.

41

Viewed as a privilege rather than a burden, the caretaker may be able to gain a deeper awareness of his own feelings about death itself.

For the dying person, life is changing. He knows that he will no longer be. That is a feeling that is experienced alone. No other person, no matter how supportive, can feel what he feels. Within this process the practitioner can develop a momentary empathy with what the patient is experiencing and they may share a brief yet powerful moment of aloneness, yet each is experiencing an aloneness known only to them as individuals. There is strength in this experience because the aloneness of dying is very intense for both. Within these moments emerge the agonies of any health care worker - the helplessness one feels while attempting to support the strengths of the person who is dying. Health care workers involved in terminal care need to allow space which accommodates the paradoxes of being together and being apart. Gibran tells us "and stand together yet not too near together; for the pillars of the temple stand apart."[14]

When we speak of aloneness, we refer to an individual uniqueness. There is a difference between being alone and being lonely. For a dying person, the aloneness that we speak of is the experience of a separateness that allows the person to be with his own feelings and his own thoughts without the intrusion of others. In this aloneness he makes his decisions to accept his own death, and he makes the ultimate choice of how to deal with it. When this separateness occurs, the patient emerges from it at a level that is not shared by either his family or the staff. At such times, conflicts may arise because, in his aloneness, he has experienced and grown from profound introspection. He is operating at a unique level of awareness, while family and staff are seeking their own separateness and their own growth.

The experience of dying is lonely. The experience of aloneness is germane to life as well as to death. It is a solo moment of intense feeling. Aloneness is a part of every human experience. Being alone, being unique and being oneself means being lonely. Moustakas describes loneliness as a condition of man: "Man is ultimately and forever lonely, whether his lonliness is the exquisite pain of the individual living in isolation or illness, the sense of absence caused by a loved one's death, or the piercing joy experienced in triumphant creation."[15]

Healthcare workers need to understand what is going on inside themselves: what makes them want to run away; what makes it difficult to be "there" in a helping relationship; what makes it painful to sustain a relationship with the dying and their families. In essence when the professional has a philosophy of life or recognizes that man is a complex unique being who is different yet similar, each with his own history, then the uniqueness of being a helper can be a tremendous experience of growth. In conjunction with Moustakas, we believe "it is necessary for every person to recognize his loneliness, to become intensely aware that, ultimately, in every fiber of his being, man is alone - terribly, utterly alone."[16]

When patient and practitioner come together, they bring to any experience their own historicity. With this in mind one can understand the need for seeking to establish a commonality of goals with a special relationship. It is a contractual arrangement in which the practitioner helps the patient by meeting his needs, insofar as possible, and the patient helps the practitioner by opening up and allowing the person to enter his world as he is experiencing it.

REFERENCES

1. Pearson, Leonard, *Death And Dying: Issues In The Treatment of The Dying Person*, The Press of Case Western Reserve University, 1969.
2. Mervyn, *The Plight of The Dying Patients In Hospitals*, The American Journal of Nursing, October, 1971.
3. Travelbee, Joyce, M.S.N., R.N., *Interpersonal Aspects of Nursing*, F.A. Davis Company, Philadelphia, PA., 1966.
4. Travelbee, Joyce, M.S.N., R.N., *Interpersonal Aspects of Nursing*, F.A. Davis Company, Philadelphia, PA., 1966.
5. Saunders, Cicely, M.D., an article by Sylvia Lack, M.D., and Anastasia Toufaxis, "Hospice: Putting More Living Into Dying," *Hospital Tribune*, Feb., 1978.
6. Zderad, Loretta T., R.N., Ph.D., *Empathetic Nursing*," Nursing Clinics of North America, Vol. 4, No. 4., W. B. Saunders Company, Philadelphia, PA., Dec. 1969
7. LeShan, Lawrence and LeShan, Eda, "Psychotherapy and the Patient With A Limited Life Span," *The Phenomenon of Death*, Harper Colophon Books, Harper and Row, Publishers, New York, 1973.
8. Gibran, Kalil, *The Prophet*, Alfred A. Knopf, New York, 1926, Thirteenth Printing, 1969.

9. Kubler-Ross, Elisabeth, M.D., Ph.D., *On Death and Dying*, MacMillan, New York, 1969.
10. Engel, George, M.D., *Grief and Grieving*, American Journal of Nursing, September, 1964.
11. Kubler-Ross, Elisabeth, M.D., Ph.D., *On Death and Dying*, MacMillan, New York, 1969.
12. Vonnegut, Kurt, Jr., *Slaughter House Five*, 1969.
13. Paterson, Josephine G., R.N., D.N.Sc.; Zderad, Loretta, R.N., Ph.D., *Humanistic Nursing*, A Wiley Biomedical Publication, John Wiley and Sons, Inc., New York, 1976.
14. Gibran, Kahlil, *The Prophet*, Alfred A. Knopf, New York, 1926; Thirteenth Printing, 1969.
15. Moustakas, Clark E., *Loneliness*, A Spectrum Book, Prentice-Hall, Inc., Englewood Cliffs, New Jersey.
16. Moustakas, Clark E., *Loneliness*, A Spectrum Book, Prentice-Hall, Inc., Englewood Cliffs, New Jersey.

PART III
PATIENT ADVOCACY

THE PROFESSIONAL

Most individuals are not taught the basic skills of how to help dying patients and their survivors. In our culture we have not been taught how to deal with feelings about our own deaths. The difficulty lies in facing the reality of one's own mortality. Unless we learn to move beyond that emotional block in our own lives, it is difficult to help another person who is in the process of dying. Professionals who work with the dying are, theoretically, most capable at helping the dying and their families to cope with the psychological stresses of terminal illness. But this is not necessarily true, since they have not been taught how to come to terms with death, their own or anyone else's. The social and professional skills of health care professionals have traditionally been focused towards curing the patient. There has been no effort, except in recent years, to prepare staffs in learning what appropriate therapeutic behavior is toward dying patients and their families. Death has always been perceived histori- cally in America as something that should not happen. Rob- inson states that "Americans tend to regard health and happiness as due conditions - illness and death are perceived as abnormal events."[1]

We reflect this attitude in our behavior towards dying patients and see death as punishment and failure. With this confusion, this lack of specific guidelines for appropriate behavior, how are professionals to know what their roles are and what their behavior should be in caring for the dying?

The patient is experiencing his own death. He has no way of knowing what his behavior should be. But, basically, he needs to find some semblance of meaning in this new experience. He needs the help of staff to enable him to do this. His needs are physical, emotional, spiritual and practical. He is dependent upon some other fellow human to help him pull these things together into some meaningful order. His struggle is the search for meaning in this experience. The dying person reaches out to others for support, guidance, understanding and answers. His needs include support as he loses everything, his life and all that his life entails. This places a tremendous responsibility on caretakers.

The role of the professional is to meet, on a daily basis, the multiple needs of the patient. Advocacy is the willingness to do for the patient and with the patient those things that are feasible that will allow the patient to move into the experience of dying unencumbered by such extraneous needs as making a will, taking care of family business and making various arrangements in order to effect closures in his life.

The role of the professional is to be the patient's advocate in terms of his rights as a patient, his desire to make a will, his need to have a say in his own funeral arrangements, his need to be understood and to maintain autonomy insofar as possible. The role of the advocate includes the setting of limits. As the patient struggles to cope with a high anxiety level, he needs professionals who anticipate and understand the overwhelming fears that the patient is confronting. The advocate represents a form of stability as the patient struggles with his emotions. The professional as advocate maintains a therapeutic position in the face of the patient's various mood swings, which means an attitude that is consistent and non-punitive. Therapeutic intervention is a position of understanding the purpose of the patient's behavior and not seeing it as a threat or rejection of one's personal self. This is often seen when a patient becomes frustrated, angry and frightened: as his behavior becomes self centered, the staff tends to isolate him. They do not understand that so much of the patient's energy is spent dealing with his emotions that he is unable to relate in "expected" ways to others. Each person has the right to deal with his own death in his own way. This behavior is part of the unique individuality of every person.

When the multidisciplinary approach is used to meet his needs, the patient may relate to one particular member of the team. In this way he may select his own therapist. The question is, will the staff member be prepared to respond in appropriate and supportive ways? This is where the team supports the person in order that a therapeutic relationship can be established and maintained. Staff attitudes need to be flexible and open in order to accomodate and to encourage this kind of interaction between patients and staff.

The advocate must determine and know "where the patient is" and "where the family is" in relation to their circumstances. Patient advocacy requires that staff intervene to help the patient and his family clarify the reality of their situation. The patient may still be active in certain decision-making processes within his family, but as family responsibilities and functions shift so does the structure of the family, which frequently leads to conflict and confusion. This is where the primary person is able to help the family sort out facts and to make plans in keeping with the reality of their circumstances. For example, a mother who organizes a home and the activities within it may have to relinquish this role to family members. They need her help, she needs their support; the advocate's role is to help the family resolve some of these issues. When there is a role change in a family through terminal illness, the role of the professional is to recognize the vast implications involved in the family structure, being sensitive to the needs of the patient as well as the family.

Having come to grips with their own deaths and having considered the importance of the role one plays in terminal care may lead to the realization that the need is for change in attitudes and behavior towards oneself in relation to the dying person. Bunch and Zahra tell us that "having considered the importance of roles, one may have the foundation needed to begin changing attitudes and behavior toward the dying patient."[2]

Everyone involved in the process of death grows as a result of sharing in this major life change. The dying person accepts his own death and now detaches himself. Family members return to continue living in a new and different way. And the professional, having shared a significant role with the family as well as the patient, grows through the changes that characterize their experiences in living and dying.

THE STAFF

Patients today are admitted to hospitals in several ways. These include entry through the emergency room, direct entry by ambulance to a ward, and entry through the admissions office. But by whatever means a person becomes a patient, the experience is traumatic and frightening. Part of the fear is based on the situation that brings the person to the hospital in the first place. A deeper fear sets in when the person finds himself to be completely out of control of his situation in terms of the things that are being done to and for his body. Whether man, woman, or child, people are accustomed to having some control over any activity that concerns the handling of their bodies. And this loss of control, however temporary, can cause severe emotional shock. The ensuing feeling of helplessness is a frightening experience to which people react in different ways. Such feelings of helplessness sometimes account for patients who cry silently in the dentist's chair even when there is no pain involved, or in the physician's office when simple procedures are causing minimal fear and no pain. To maintain some control over one's body is a basic need and is essential to emotional equilibrium. When a person becomes a patient, this basic right is forfeited.

When the patient is terminal, not only is he no longer in control of what is happening to him; not only are families caught up in how a negative prognosis threatens, affects and changes their lives; they are forced to deal with feelings that frequently they don't even understand. The problems begin with the illness, they increase with hospitalization and escalate with the diagnosis that the patient's condition is terminal. But it is important to be aware that the problems faced by terminal patients and their families are initiated long before the person is diagnosed as terminal. The stress and the related problems are initiated at the point that illness can no longer be denied and hospitalization is required, for it is at this point that not only is it necessary for the patient to relinquish control of himself; so must the family relinquish its autonomy regarding the course of his care. Both patient and family become dependent upon strangers in an unfamiliar setting to provide for his needs, to hopefully save his life, to provide information and offer comfort and hope. How well these human needs are recognized and met will determine the extent of the problems for patient, family and staff.

When we speak of patient-family problems in relation to staff and how these problems are met or "dealt" with, it is usually within the context of (acting-out) behavior and ("negative") attitudes. It is necessary to understand at the outset that terminal illness is much more than a threat to the patient's life. It is a disruptive force to the person's total way of life, and to the lives of his or her family unit. It is a destructive force to all that the person has or hoped to accomplish. It prompts a special terror all its own. And when this extreme but normal emotion is compounded by the fears, the rules and regulations of hospitalization with its unknowns, the need to surrender one's independence, social identity and personal autonomy, the problems of patient and family will emerge to challenge the staff. Terminal illness presents a gigantic, unwelcomed interruption to the personal script that the person has been involved in as a way of life. And over this revision of plans, the patient has no control.

Today, when we hear that someone is terminal, the usual question that follows is "does he know?" or "does she know?" By contrast to earlier times when people gathered in the home at the bedside of a dying person as a pattern of conduct, today many people find excuses to stay away: "I just can't bring myself to go;" "I don't want to see him or her that way;" "I don't know what to say." People justify their behavior in terms of the dread and unpleasantness of the situation. It is not a pleasant experience to witness the course of death. But the real reason is fear—fear of death, fear of feelings of inadequacy to change things, fear of knowing one is helpless to control the situation of pain and suffering, fear of facing the reminder of one's own mortality, fear of not knowing how to relate to the dying, and fear of not knowing what constitutes appropriate behavior.

These are some of the reasons that friends and families sometimes avoid a loved one who is dying. These emotions are very similar to the feelings of caretakers who have no choice but to be involved with dying patients on some level each day. Many caretakers share feelings similar to these. As death becomes imminent, there is an increased risk that the distance will become more pronounced between patient and staff, patient and family, and patient and friends. It is at this point in the course of terminal illness that the patient's worst fears might be realized, and that is the fear of being abandoned, of being left to die alone.

Health care workers who learn to cope successfully with uncomfortable feelings about dying patients are able to establish therapeutic relationships with patients and families that are also rewarding for the practitioners. Learning to cope does not mean learning not to feel. It means learning to become aware of one's own feelings, to acknowledge those feelings, to understand one's own emotions, and finally, to accept and cope with them. Patients need help; families need help; and health care practitioners need help if they are to provide effective therapeutic intervention and support on a

51

daily basis. Without appropriate training and support for staff, there is the high risk of emotional "burn out." Without appropriate training, self-awareness and built-in support systems, even the most dedicated practitioners will be unable to sustain high quality performance in terminal care for very long, as far as the patients' psychological needs are concerned. When "all hope is gone" in terms of staff's efforts to restore the health of the patient's physical self, the quality of emotional support will make the total effort seem more worthwhile.

Think of the basic need to treat the total person. It is not sufficient to attend to the physical aspects of a person and not consider the emotional quality as well. Imagine that you are the assigned social worker, or the nurse on the ward where a terminal patient has been admitted for care. What will you do for the patient? How will you approach the situation? What are your goals and what do you hope to accomplish? What can you do to help someone who is going to die? What would a person who is in the process of dying want you to do? How can you determine what his or her needs are?

You feel frightened, awkward, confused and uncertain, but you are willing to try. You are aware of being afraid, but do you know why you are so fearful? Can you touch the place in your body where the tension has mounted? You probably can, but you still feel scared because despite all else, your role is not clear. What is expected of you? What do you expect of yourself? And, what do you expect of the patient? You can be reasonably sure that he or she is experiencing the fears and anxieties you have read about, and we have mentioned only a few. There are many others. But think again of yourself. How do you approach this situation? First of all, determine and clarify your basic role with the patient as you perceive it. Try to assume an attitude of openness and a willingness to learn and change.

Your role as a health care practitioner in terminal care is to help meet the special needs of people who are dying. These needs will be both physical and emotional. They will require both task-oriented activities and others that are primarily emotionally supportive. The role of the social worker will best be met through services of therapeutic intervention, or supportive treatment as a primary goal. These include the need to help patient and family work through feelings and to resolve problems of a practical nature. The role of the nurse will include both physical and emotional aspects of treatment goals. Remember that what is happening to the patient is also affecting his family, and their ability to deal with the problems will affect the patient whose concern for them is still a significant part of his life.

The medical aspect of the patient's treatment plan will present less of a problem to the staff since it is more highly organized and well-defined. The physician determines the course of treatment, and the nurses assist the physicians in carrying out the treatment plans. It is documented, as are the follow-through and the outcome which holds the staff accountable for compliance. This is the significant difference between the physical care that terminal patients receive and the emotional support that they require (which may or may not be consistently provided). Under most prevailing circumstances, if therapeutic intervention is available at all, it is most often provided in a helter-skelter fashion and with great inconsistencies, which is one of the major problems in terminal care in America today. It is an unfavorable condition which can have negative effects on patients, their families and staff alike.

In order to meet the needs of terminal patients and their families, we must first learn to listen. We must learn to "hear" what the patient means by what he or she is saying. Patients, if given the opportunity, will tell us what their needs are. For example, a patient who says to you "I am going to die, but I don't want my wife to know," might actually be asking you to: (1) help him to find the strength to talk with his wife about it; (2) support him after he tells her; and (3) help them to deal with it while they go through the ordeal of his illness. A wife on the other hand might ask you not to let her husband know that she knows he is going to die. She might actually be saying to you: (1) please help me to handle this; (2) help me to share this pain with my husband; (3) give me some guidelines as to how I can approach him about it; (4) will you stand by to help me throughout this ordeal?; (5) I am afraid; (6) What if I cry? Is that all right?; (7) Will you be available to help me when I need you?

Remember that each patient is an invididual and circumstances vary. The approach to one situation will not necessarily be the best approach for another despite the obvious similarities in the different situations. Learning to listen to patients and to hear what they actually mean by what they say will enable you to learn to identify with what they are experiencing. Patients can best tell us what their problems are.

The third-ear principle is the art of hearing what is meant by what was said. In good communication with terminal patients, it is the art of learning to listen purposefully. It is learning to train your ears to hear what people actually mean by what they say no matter how subtle the expression. This technique will enable you to identify with what terminal patients are experiencing. It will enable you to determine with them, by process of clarification, what their essential needs are and what can be done about them. Empathy then becomes a distinct possibility. But listening well to the patient is only one major part of the process. It is just as necessary to observe as it is to hear. Maintain eye contact with the person and use your own senses of sight and sound to tune in to the emotions and needs of dying patients. The combination of listening and looking will be the barometer by which you measure the feelings of the patient. It is essential to learning to identify your own feelings.

When properly developed, this is the skill that will make it possible for you to engage in human-to-human interaction with people who are dying. It is within this therapeutic atmosphere that you will become able to perceive their needs and to formulate realistic and practical plans to meet them. You will begin to internalize your role as a health care practitioner in meeting the needs of dying patients to the best of your ability. You will begin to discover your own depths for empathetic involvement, your own skills for becoming effectively therapeutic, your own level of strength and tolerance, and finally, appreciation for the rewarding realization that your unique contributions to the life of someone who is dying are significant.

In the meantime, how do you begin to do what must be done to meet the special needs of dying patients? That is the difficult part. It is much more difficult to reach the point of saying "I can." Let us begin by examining a hypothetical situation:

A 36 year old patient has been admitted to the ward and diagnosed as having cancer of the lung - prognosis negative.

He has family and friends who visit, but his depression is most obvious after they have gone. You want to help him. What would you do? You have two options: (1) You could talk to him; or (2) You could avoid talking to him. Talking in this sense does not mean the "Hi, how are you today?" kind of approach that is meant to establish superficial communication. By talking we mean a goal-directed approach that can be meaningful, productive and sustained to a point of therapeutic significance. Learn now to identify and acknowledge whatever feeling your body is experiencing. Your body is responding to what you are thinking. Be honest with emotions and ask yourself...What am I thinking at this moment? What am I feeling? Am I afraid to talk with this patient? Why am I afraid? What about this patient is frightening to me? Your fears could include such things as: (1) being afraid of not knowing what to say; (2) fear of saying it the wrong way; (3) being afraid of what the patient might say; (4) fear that you won't know how to respond to what the patient might say; (5) fear that the patient might tell you he is dying; (6) if he does what do you say?; (7) you might be afraid to simply walk into a room to talk with a person who is going to die; (8) You might be afraid that you are risking yourself too much; (9) What if the patient rejects you? What if I upset this patient? What if the patient asks me something that I don't know?

If these are some of the fearsome thoughts that are floating around in your mind, your body will respond by becoming very tense. You might even get a headache. These frequent conditions of stress in caretakers account for the isolation of dying patients, and no wonder! Who wants to experience such discomfort if you don't have to? But in fact, the stress is there before you have even entered the patient's room. So what is the problem here? Your approach is the problem. The many negative feelings regarding death and dying can assure that the self-fulfilling prophecy of failure to communicate will occur.

Let's begin again with your having a better idea of what your role is in terminal care. To be therapeutically helpful to dying patients, your first approach will be to get in touch with what you are feeling about death. You will need to determine goals. What do you hope to accomplish by talking with a terminal patient? Your immediate goals might include introducing yourself, asking the patient how you might help, assuring him of your availability to help him, to talk with him whenever he feels the need, *relating to him as a person who is confined to the hospital and not as a person who is going to die.* Your role is to help him to live as best he can.

It is how well he is able to live that should concern you. His dying will take care of itself. He does not know you. Do not try to rush the relationship. In or out of hospitals, establishment of sound relationships take time. Your role includes the need to be respectful. Allow the patient to move at his own pace. Be aware of behavior that might be misconstrued by sensitive patients. If his name is Tom Charles, refer to him as Mr. Charles, despite his youth or advanced age, unless and until he specifically asks you to call him by his first name, and despite the manner in which he might be referred to by your co-workers. You are new to this person. Perhaps he has asked other staff members to call him Tom. Give him the benefit of the doubt. Your initial approach to establishing a therapeutic relationship with a person who is terminal is not "I need to know so much," "what will I say if," "suppose he," or "what will I do" kind of confusion that it might seem to be. The patient is a person with needs. You are a practitioner in the position of helping to meet some of those needs. You are not expected to become a super social worker or a super nurse or a super person. You need only to become aware that you are in a human to human relationship that is a very normal circumstance of life.

The following hypothetical situation is "your first" involvement with a terminal patient. Reflect on the things you have learned so far in relation to yourself, your feelings and needs; then think of the needs and feelings of this young terminal patient. Put yourself in the role of working with him and try to determine what you will discover about yourself.

If you believe that the thirty-six year old man who is dying of cancer on your ward would benefit from therapeutic intervention, what would you do? You have never before talked to anyone who is dying. You have never been requested to assist, in any capacity, a patient who is diagnosed as terminal. But through your daily activities on the ward you have heard about the patient whose x-ray reports revealed that his cancer of the lung was rapidly metastasising. You are aware of the medical opinion that he might live from six months to one year. While working with other patients, you have observed him with friends who visit from time to time. You have noticed his sadness and how terribly alone he seems to be.

You feel that he needs someone to talk with him about his problems. You have seen other staff members performing various medical procedures, but you have seen no one on the staff talking to him about his problems and his feelings. You feel uncomfortable just saying hello and moving on. You want to help him but you don't know how. You don't know what to do or say. You mention him to a co-worker and you say how terrible it must be for him. "He's the youngest patient on the ward, and he's going to die." Then you add, "He needs someone to talk to. I can tell. I wish I could help him." The process has begun. Your wish to help him has activated your desire to do something for him. You need someone to tell you how. But no one on the ward is aware of your need to reach out to help Tom, and you feel too unsure of yourself to approach him about his problems, so what do you do?

First of all you can begin by establishing support systems for yourself. Inform the head nurse and the physician of your concern about the patient. Share your feelings about him with members of your ward team. Discuss the situation with them to gain information as well as to inform them of what you know about the patient. Share with others your ideas of what goals might be selected for helping this patient. Get feedback on your ideas. By doing this you have already encouraged teamwork to meet this patient's emotional needs. By sharing your intentions with staff, you have let others know of your interest and have provided groundwork for getting support as you become involved with the patient on a therapeutic level. Other staff members are not unaware of his depression. Like you they may be reluctant to become involved in the patient's emotions. As you become the patient's advocate, staff will not only support you, they most likely will reinforce you by joining and sharing your efforts. Others might begin to pay a bit more attention to Tom while performing routine medical procedures. Most health care practitioners want to do more to help terminal patients to deal with their emotional pain, but fear and uncertainty prevent them from extending their efforts to try.

The most difficult part is over at the moment you decide to reach out to a terminal person. With staff encouragement, you are better prepared to become therapeutically involved with a dying patient. You are afraid, but you are willing to try. No one can teach another to effectively work with the dying. Like learning anything else, the skills develop from motivation, persistence and desire to grow. Students and people new to terminal care need assurance that they will not cause the patient any harm. It is helpful to give this assurance because it is a natural tendency to fear "doing or saying the wrong thing."

In case you still feel uneasy about the prospect of not doing something right, let's examine the situation further before you enter the patient's room. Remind yourself that it is your desire to help this patient. You want to talk to him for some of the following purposes. You are: (1) letting him know that you are aware of his presence; (2) wanting him to know that you want to help him; (3) wanting to know how you might help him; (4) assuring him that help is available according to his physical and emotional needs; (5) helping him to feel more secure and comfortable because through you he can become more aware that the staff is concerned for his care and comfort; (6) giving him dignity by showing him that you and staff are aware of his needs for support; (7) giving him the courage to reach out when he needs support and a willingness to respond when support is offered; (9) introducing him to a more therapeutic environment in which he can find solace in the midst of crushing emotional pain; (10) becoming a significant ally; (11) helping him to feel better because you are there; (12) assuring him that he will not be abandoned; (13) supporting his strengths and his hopes for recovery.

How do you do all of these things? You begin by admitting to yourself (and to some supportive team member) that you are afraid. You might find that your fear of death is not as great as your desire to help this patient who is dying. Identify in your body where the fear has caused the greatest tension. Touch the fear by placing your hand on your head, your stomach, your throat or wherever the tension is most concentrated. Having located and acknowledged the fear, take a deep breath and say to yourself audibly: "I am scared, but I am going to talk with Tom because I believe I can help him. I want to help him. I believe that I can." At that point, you summon sufficient courage to go directly to the patient to talk with him as a person. Nothing could be more human. And in no way will you do him harm. Approach him the same way you would any other patient. He will help you to help him. Be natural. Be yourself.

Fear of death is only one barrier to good terminal care. Fear of doing the wrong thing or saying the wrong thing is a major concern for both experienced and inexperienced caretakers. Fear becomes constructive in terminal care only when it is based on the possibility that because of fear, help for dying people can be denied them. There is little need to fear that you might cause them harm when your goal is to be therapeutic.

Clarified, your role is: (1) to become the patient's advocate in a strange and artificial, frightening and impersonal environment; (2) to talk with the patient to provide information that is relevant and appropiate; (3) to listen to what the patient wants to say; (4) to be available; (5) to share relevant and appropriate information with staff in order to mutually seek solutions to the patient's problems; (6) to help the patient and the family to deal with their real problems in a goal-directed way. Remind yourself that you are not going in to talk with Tom about death. But if he mentions it your role is to hear what he says, allow him to express his feelings and assure him of your desire to help him in any way possible. Your role is to communicate with him about your plans in relation to his presence. The first impression will be long-lasting. Your initial visit might accomplish no more than the wish in the patient's mind that you come to see him again. Rapport in terminal patient care is established as gradually as it is in regular patient care. If you are in touch with your feelings, clear in your purposes and sincere in you intentions, it will be reflected in your attitude and approach. The patient will perceive the positive quality of your efforts and will accept you as an ally. You will have established the foundation upon which a therapeutic relationship can develop. You will feel good about yourself. And you should share the experience with co-workers who are interested in your efforts.

A major barrier to good terminal care is that health care practitioners do not have a clear understanding of their roles with dying patients in terms of the patient's emotional needs. Caretakers frequently state that the problem is the "lack of sufficient time" to do therapeutic intervention. While this excuse might be realistic for various reasons (i.e. insufficient staff) it is not the primary condition that contributes to the emotional neglect of dying patients.

The basic reason is fear of one's own unresolved feelings about death. Other causes are related to the confusion about what a truly therapeutic relationship in terminal care involves and who should enter into it. It is not a role for exclusive assignment to any one profession. Nurses who work intimately with patient's physical needs on a daily basis are in ideal positions to communicate with dying patients on therapeutic levels. Meaningful dialogue is possible while patients are being turned, bathed, or having their skin massaged with lotion. Therapeutic intervention is not dependent upon long, time-consuming discussions. The nurse who is tuned into the patient's emotional needs can be effectively therapeutic while performing tasks that require only a few minutes if the nurse is able to "hear" and to respond to emotional needs according to what the patient is saying.

To be effective, a therapeutic environment requires input from everyone who works with the patient in any capacity. Therapeutic intervention is the ability and the willingness to respond appropriately to what the patient is experiencing. For instance a reply of "don't worry about it," is not a therapeutic response to the patient who says, "I'll probably lose my job. The doctor says I'll be in here for a while." A social worker's appropriate response would be: "Let's talk about that. Perhaps I can help you with this problem." The patient and the social worker can then work together to find solutions to this situation. A nurse's appropriate response would be: "I understand how that must worry you. Would you care to discuss the situation with the social worker? Perhaps you can work something out with your employer. I'll ask the social worker to come in and talk with you." One professional's role complements the other in a therapeutic environment. Knowing one's own role in relation to another's and having respect for mutual and different aspects of role assignment is what makes teamwork function.

Multidisciplinary teamwork in terminal care is the best

method to ensure *that patient/family needs are known and met to the fullest extent possible.* It also is a method by which the staff learns to be supportive to each other. Staff needs, when met in terminal care, will strongly influence the degree to which patient/family concerns are given realistic, professional and effective consideration. Through regular team sessions, the staff comes closer together as a mutual support system. Team planning allows staff to become more responsive to each other's needs while providing quality services to the dying patients and their families.

THE FAMILY

Almost nobody dies at home anymore. Within the past 75 years, health care for serious illness has become hospital oriented. With rare exceptions, patients admitted to hospitals and diagnosed as terminal will either die there or in alternative nursing care facilities. Until the turn of the century in our country, most people died at home, and consequently there was more family involvement in the care and treatment of dying patients. Neighbors and friends were available to help however they could, and survivors actively shared the burdens of decision-making and responsibilities during the terminal illness of a relative.

With the advent of modern medical technology which provides us with life saving and life sustaining devices, many choices in health care that were previously the prerogatives of next of kin have been relinquished. Families and patients alike have of necessity given up control in many decision-making matters, since certain medical procedures are possible only within the confines of hospitals and related health care facilities. The major responsibility has shifted from home to hospital. But the provision of physical hospital care, however admirable, if untouched by *consistent* consideration for the psychological well-being of terminal patients, is no longer sufficient. Healthcare workers in hospitals have now become a significant support system for the family of the terminally ill. The trauma of terminal illness is compounded by the stress of being in a hospital environment, separated from the familiar comfort of one's own bed and one's own home with all the familiar sights and sounds and smells of one's family's daily activities. These comforts and trusted support systems are lost to the patient. Lost to the family are

61

the well-established patterns which allowed them to provide for the sick relative in a familiar environment where they had full control of decisions that a family makes when a disruption occurs or when a crisis must be faced such as caring for a dying loved one.

Due to the reality of complex medical problems, procedures and modern technology so necessary in caring for the dying, hospitalization at some stage of a person's illness becomes a necessary aspect in terminal care. Hospitals are typically identified as places of illness and human suffering. But, despite this negative connotation, the history of hospitals is hardly worthy of such descriptions as sad and depressing places. Hospitals were born as a testament of man's humanity to man. But in order for families to realize the benefits that hospitals can offer, help from a sensitive staff is needed to enable both patient and family to negotiate the complex system of bureaucracy that is characteristic of any hospitalization.

The need for hospitalization is a stressful situation even under the best of circumstances and conditions. And for terminal patients and their families, that problems are to be anticipated should be a foregone conclusion. Families experience episodes of grief and need to work through their feelings and to grow through the experience in ways very similar to the emotional stages that the patients struggle through. The difference is that sometimes the patient might work through his emotional pain in a way (and with nature's help) that allows him to eventually accept his death. The family must learn to survive the loss. Families are challenged to regroup and recover in a way that will allow the family unit to continue despite the irreversible void that is created by the death of one of its members. The family will never be the same. The prospect of death, with its subsequent changes within the family, is incomprehensible to them, but they must mobilize their strengh and learn to change and to grow and to survive as a family unit despite the pain which accompanies these circumstances.

A wife who sits all day at the hospital with her dying husband is meeting some of his needs, and she is also meeting certain needs of her own. Once she leaves the hospital she must continue to deal with needs of her own on a different level. She is forced to ponder her own life and the drastic changes occurring within it. She must also cope with the responsibility of maintaining stability within the home when children are involved.

This need to maintain a constant bedside vigil is frequently shared by the whole family. The motives for this behavior need to be understood by the staff, who might be overwhelmed by sheer numbers. This need for family members to congregate around the dying member is sometimes representative of their needs to deny that death is occurring, to come together as a unit for strength, to offer support to the dying, and to maintain for as long as they can family togetherness as a unit while the dying relative is still among them. In certain ethnic groups it is traditional for family members to come together to celebrate certain events. These include birth, weddings, christenings, *bar mitzvahs* and other celebrated occasions—including the death of a family member. But often relatives are unable to cope and may withdraw from the dying relative because they cannot tolerate the presence of death.

While families are experiencing the various stages of grief, and when denial is strong, family members may be unable to visit the patient. They may find communication difficult and even embarrassing. At this stage a relative might inappropriately suggest that the terminal patient is "the picture of health," or make some statement to the effect that the patient will be "up and out of here in no time," when they both know that the real issue is being avoided. Families have great difficulty accepting the prospect of death and the fact that their life as a family will never again be the same. They continue to hope against all odds that somehow he or she will get well and return to the family unit and that the family will remain the same. Loss connotes change and change connotes never being the same. What is known feels secure and a death in the family reminds us of the impermanence of human life—our own as well as those we love. It is difficult to lose a loved one and more difficult to know what is appropriate behavior in the midst of impending loss. The pain of loss through death is the reality that a part of us dies with each significant death, expecially among family members.

What is our expectation for behavior in family members who are in the process of losing a loved one? Some family members suffer silently because the rules in their family have been that to show emotion is a weakness. One "must be strong and keep a stiff upper lip." These are the families who say "we are managing all right." These are the people who resort to teasing and joking as a means of communication among themselves and with the staff. This behavior is their way of coping with deep emotional pain. It is not an invitation for either the patient or the staff to join in a mutual exchange of merriment and joviality. It is a plea for help and understanding. Healthcare workers need to respond to the *unspoken needs* of patients and families rather than to their style of expressing their needs and feelings.

Some families have a unique way of communicating with each other that is understood only by them. This is the pattern of behavior that might continue between them under all conditions. For example, a man and woman who have never communicated with each other on an honest and open level during 39 years of marriage will not automatically change their method of communication when one or the other is diagnosed as terminal. For the most part people die as they have lived. More than likely, they will relate to each other in a pattern of communication that is mutually understood by both of them, even in the face of death, as they have done in the entirety of their lives together. The staff cannot change this, but needs to be aware of the ways in which families relate to each other and function as a unit.

A 57 year old man complained to the staff that his wife had not been informed that she had terminal cancer. He insisted that he knew only because the doctors had told him but he could not talk with his wife about it and that he felt helpless to help her as he wanted to because the doctors "had not told her." During therapeutic intervention it was learned that both knew that she was terminal but it could not be openly discussed. And the reason for this, as it developed, was that the communication between this couple had for 37 years been based on avoidance of issues. They had never directly verbalized their feelings and thoughts openly to each other on any serious matter. Many families relate to each other with incongruent or double level messages. This pattern of metacommunication in families is what accounts for their ways of behaving towards each other in a manner not necessarily understood by outsiders. Every family is unique in the way they function in health and during periods of stress.

It should not be assumed, therefore, that a relative who does not visit a terminal family member is uncaring. Each survivor is unique within his own needs and responses to existing circumstances. Many families do share their grief, but it is important to know that each family member also grieves alone. Each needs certain support systems. For example, emotional support within certain families is often sufficient during the crisis of a terminal illness, especially in families where open communication of thoughts and feelings represent their normal way of life. On the other hand, there are some families who are unable to express feelings to each other and who might benefit more from therapeutic intervention from a health care worker. This is seen sometimes, for example, in a family that has suffered the loss of a child. Such a loss can foster closeness or it can present overwhelming marital difficulties. Grieving families each experience the loss of a loved one in a different way. Oftentimes, the dying person moves toward acceptance long before the family is either aware of it or able to let go. Families continue to live because they are survivors, but the memory of the lost loved one remains as evidenced by the trauma of experiencing those first anniversaries of significant occasions which they shared in the past. We often hear "this is the first Thanksgiving without John" or "Alice would have liked this day so much because she always looked forward to trimming the Christmas tree." The widow who remarries but still speaks often of her deceased husband is an example of the difficulty of adjustment to loss. Adjustment in relation to loss is a gradual process. It is not easy for families to accept the fact that the process of dying that their loved one is experiencing will lead to his actual death, and to irreversible loss in their own lives. When a family is facing the loss of a significant person, behavior that might otherwise be seen as erratic is really within normal range.

As families grieve it is important for them to be part of the care of the dying patient, performing such things as bathing, shaving, feeding, and grooming the sick relative. Staff needs to understand the needs of family members to be part of the terminal care of their loved one. A relative who is allowed to bathe a loved one, to feed and to make him comfortable in various ways is able to retain some feelings of

65

control, usefulness and autonomy. Health care workers who recognize stress, whether subtle or overt, and who are able to respond to the family's needs are more helpful to patients, families and staff. Ideally, this significant triad combines to cope with the process of dying and to help each other in meeting basic common human needs that are inherent in effective terminal care.

"Before I can teach children about death, someone has to straighten me out!"[3]

EMOTIONAL NEEDS OF CHILDREN

In years past, a dying member of the family was surrounded by neighbors, friends and family who knew and loved him. These gatherings frequently included children. Family closeness was a source of support and understanding while providing an opportunity for the children to learn first hand about significant aspects of life. Within this family structure they were able to form basic attitudes about life and death. Stannard tells us that the Puritan child not only learned about death very early, but was taught to fear it. By contrast, children of the nineteenth century were taught to look forward to death and the ultimate reunion with loved ones.[4] Today families are separated by distance and changing attitudes towards living and dying. For example, children today are protected from death rather than being part of the dying process of a loved one. This development in our society causes us to ignore or fail to recognize the needs of children when death occurs.

A child who experiences a loss through death is caught in a terrible state of confusion with feelings of discomfort over which he has no control. The child is unable to handle these emotions unless he has help from someone who is sensitive enough to recognize his needs and caring enough to reach out to him. Management of a child's stress is the responsibility of adults. Children's needs for appropriate support through feelings of anxiety, panic, shame, guilt and fury are very realistic responsibilities of adults. Redl supports the thinking that these are feelings that children experience, and emotions with which they are unable to cope.[5] The support of adults is crucial to the emotional well-being of children who mourn.

The most effective teachers, counselors, and caretakers in the area of helping others to deal with death and dying are the people who have themselves clarified their own thinking, attitudes, and feelings about death in general and about their own mortality in particular. This is true in helping adults, and even more so in helping children. Today, many children are excluded, shielded and protected by adults because they, themselves, are unable to deal openly and honestly with feelings about death. This is unfortunate since children cannot in reality be protected from death, nor can they be spared the emotional pain and anguish that is caused by death. It is a disservice to mislead children about death, a fact of life which they must confront throughout their own lives. The information and attitudes about death provided to children at an early age will determine the attitudes that shape their lives as adults. If negative, it is an unnecessary burden which can be avoided. Through honest, sensitive and informed staff, parents and other responsible adults who deal with children, they can be helped to form healthy attitudes about living and dying.

Children are not as fragile as many adults imagine them to be. They are stronger and more capable of handling truth and unpleasant situations than generally thought. Children are observant, curious, perceptive and sensitive to the emotions of adults around them and under conditions of emotional stress, when attitudes of grownups change, children are aware, whether they question the situation or not. The truth, in almost any situation, when handled with sensitivity, consistency and concern, can be more easily dealt with by children and adults alike. Deliberate efforts to obscure the truth generates confusion, fear and feelings of discomfort which can be damaging to the inquisitive and highly imaginative minds of children who need the trust and support of responsible, mature adults especially during these highly stressful periods in their lives. Children should not be told that death is "like falling asleep." People who thoughtlessly explain death to children this way later wonder why they have difficulty falling asleep, suffer loss of appetite, or spend restless nights filled with nightmares and other nocturnal discomforts such as bedwetting.

As Elizabeth Reed says, being available to children, listening to them, encouraging questions and being sensitive to their feelings with an openness for further conversation about death, can help assure that children's fears and anxieties about death will not be pushed back to become buried in their subconscious and cause disturbances in later years.[6]

It is not uncommon for children to ask probing questions about death. Long before many parents are aware of it, very young children observe and participate in the process of death and dying on a daily basis. They observe, for instance, what happens to a swatted fly or a sprayed cockroach, they step on ants and bugs on sidewalks while walking or playing with friends, or see dead dogs and cats on roads and highways. Their curiosities raise such questions as: "Is that dog dead?" The parent probably is able to acknowledge that it is but if the child then asks "What is death?" the parent may avoid a direct answer and talk instead about the dangers of playing in the street. The child's question prompts fear in the parents about death as well as the safety and well-being of the child. And a moment goes unrecognized as an opportunity to teach a child about death. A parent could perhaps say simply that death is when all life has left the body. Reed explains that very often a child's first experience in facing death occurs when a pet dies. The child loves the pet, grieves for it and is concerned about what happens to it.[7]

Children are individuals and unique in their learning experiences. While it might prompt a series of additional questions from others, children's questions should be answered when asked. Answers should be given in direct, honest and simple terms. Children do not want, nor are they (like adults) prepared for, a dissertation in response to a simple question. Adults need to be curious about the kinds of questions children ask. This allows us to enter into the world of the child as he is experiencing it. Frequently the child's immediate need is not an intellectual explanation in answer to his question but an unexpressed need for reassurance and emotional security. Beneath a child's questions about death often lies anxiety or fear; fear that those he loves and who care for him may die and he will be left alone. Our first response needs to be one of understanding and reassurance. Perhaps we could bring his anxiety into the open by saying, "Why do you ask?" "What are you thinking right now?" Such a response, in addition to an honest answer to his question, provides the opportunity for communication between the adult and child for strengthening the relationship and can be beneficial in many ways.

Stefanics describes the relationship of two people as a shared growth experience "by entering into the world of the other as he reveals himself to me, I come to know him and myself in a new and different way, the experience being unique only for that particular moment in my life."[8] Children reveal their uniqueness through sharing their fantasies and thoughts. It is not unusual for young children to fantasize about death. Parents and adults who listen to a child describe his experiences or thoughts about death will come to know him as he reveals his concerns. The more sensitive and imaginative the child, the more likely he is to imagine elaborate scenes of deaths. Such thoughts involve his parents, one or both; and what is to become of him in such an event? He imagines his own death and the pain and suffering his parents will experience. Certain children entertaining these death thoughts experience real grief and actual tears while caught up in the emotions of their own fantasies. These exercises in youthful introspection are neither uncommon nor harmful to most children. They need only the sight of their parents or the sound of their voices to break the spell of their emotional self-indulgences.

Children have many thoughts and deep feelings about death and their curiosity knows no bounds. Their curiosity increases as real life experiences occur. Children's fears are frequently not expressed. They worry in silence and sometimes over long periods of time. Sometimes those closest to a child may not recognize the anxiety a child is experiencing. Reed suggests that parents will help their children in facing death if they can talk naturally with them about it before an emotional crisis arises.[9]

A child in an environment of openness and sharing about death will develop healthy attitudes as he moves through his own process of growth and development. In the absence of honest discussions about death, a child will misinterpret cliches that most adults understand. For instance, a seven year old girl was tearfully studying a calendar shortly after her father's funeral. When asked what she was searching for, she stated that she was "trying to find the date of judgement day." She had been told by a neighbor, after asking "Will I ever see my father again" that "Yes, she would see her father on judgement day." The child made a literal interpretation of this reply. Such efforts, however well intended, only hurt and confuse children who are already confused and experiencing great emotional trauma. This is supported by Reed who states that children should be told the truth. When a loved one dies, a child needs to know that he was loved but that person cannot come back to him. The child can accept this explanation better than being left with the feeling that the person he loved did not care enough and has deserted him or "gone away" without telling him goodbye.[10]

Adults who have learned to respect and value children will allow them to grow and develop in their own unique ways. Dealing with children is a two-way process which requires mutual interaction between the adult and the child. Through this open interaction, death can be discussed as a natural phenomenon of all living things in nature. Adults who work with children also need to be aware of what death means to children of different ages. Reed refers to Sylvia Anthony, who was the first investigator to work directly with children in a study of their understanding of death. She made a study of children between the ages of three and twelve years, and found that death thoughts are frequent in children of school age; they appear in children's fantasies, in their play, and in their response to suggestions of fear and separation. She learned that children between five and six years begin to have some idea of the meaning of death; by seven years their concept is much more advanced; between eight and nine years they have some logical and biological understanding; and at twelve they are beginning to develop a more mature concept.[11]

It is not uncommon for young children, while playing alone, to close their eyes and imagine themselves dead; some hold their breath to make the fantasy more real. They seldom share these solitary games with their playmates or parents because the fear of separation which prompts these games is too great and too threatening to verbalize. It is as difficult, however, for children to "get into the role" or "feel" themselves dead as it is for adults. This is understandable in view of the fact that they are observing themselves under very "unlikely" circumstances. It 'feels' like play acting. It is a more realistic experience of emotional pain when a child imagines the deaths of his mother or father or both because the threat of separation and fear of being abandoned 'feels' more real to the child, which explains perhaps why a child is easily reduced to tears while fantasizing the deaths of his parents.

A healthy situation for parents, teachers and other significant adults who spend time with children is to encourage them to express their feelings. Children, after all, live in a world of feeling and the need for self-expression and reassurance cannot be over-emphasized.

One young boy grew up haunted by the fear of death whenever he did anything that he felt would not meet with his mother's approval. When he asked her questions about death, she misused the opportunity to frighten the child into obeying her strict orders and stern code of behavior. She told him with straight face and ominous voice that death meant that he would stop breathing, be thrown into a deep dark hole in the ground to be covered up with dirt and to burn in hell if he ever misbehaved, disobeyed her, and, as she put it, "was a bad boy." She succeeded in frightening the child so much that even the most innocent childhood pranks such as eating candy before dinner caused him to spend restless nights.

Children tend to reflect the attitudes of people around them including attitudes about death. In families where emotions are expressed, where children are allowed, when a loved one dies, to see parents cry, grieve and recover, children learn that in spite of the pain involved, the family will survive.

Children should be allowed to cry when a death occurs that affects them. They need to be held and comforted and to have the opportunity to ask questions and to express their feelings no matter at what age. Telling a child not to cry, that "your mother (or your father or whomever the child is grieving for) would not want you to carry on this way" is a disservice to any grief-stricken child. It is, however unintentional, a denial of the child's right to feel and experience the pain and emotional suffering caused by the loss which, after all, is very real. A three year old girl was able to grieve with the rest of the family as well as close friends when her mother died. She was told immediately of her mother's death, why her mother had died and that the mother would not be back. It was carefully explained to her by a favorite, trusted and loving friend, that the mother loved her very much and knew that she (the child) loved her too. The child was provided whatever information she needed and asked for in an open and simple manner, in sequences and amounts as she needed it. She understood it, grieved, sought support and responded to comfort in much the same way as did the rest of the family.

A ten year old girl was so grief-stricken and bewildered at the death of her twenty-three year old sister that she feared each birthday until she was well past her twenty-third birthday. It was years later that she shared her fears of being destined to die at the same age. Adults need to be more aware of the emotional needs of children when death occurs in the family. Children need to be allowed to hear and encouraged to participate in family discussions about death in order to clarify some of their ideas about what has happened. They need to express their secret thoughts, fears and feelings. They can benefit from being taught basic things in nature in order to develop an early concept about change. Children, if taught at an early age, can comprehend that everyone is affected by change, and they can learn to perceive change in a positive way.

A perceptive mother whose precocious ten year old daughter was concerned because she was much taller than her friends, and often teased by them about her height, helped the child to gain confidence and self-esteem by introducing her to a carefully selected book of fairy tales. The little girl discovered a positive concept of change through the story of the "ugly caterpiller." She was fascinated by learning of the metamorphisis that changed it into a beautiful butterfly. The child was helped not only to grasp the significance of change, but was able to relate to the excitement of anticipating good things that happen in nature through change. Children who are taught that changes are inevitable for all things in nature will be better able to accept death as a part of this concept.

Children are society's most precious resources. They need nurturing, protection and the opportunity to grow and develop to their full potential. If they are included in discussions that affect their lives, according to their age levels, emotional maturity and curiosities, they can become more adaptable to reality. When children ask questions about death, they need sensible answers. Parents and other responsible adults are challenged to become more knowledgeable regarding how their own insecurities and fears can adversely affect children. Parents who are unable to discuss death and dying with their children can help them to learn through alternative means. Elizabeth Reed suggests the following activities: "(1) Watching seeds sprout; (2) observing a caterpillar becoming a butterfly; (3) looking at nature films; (4) making microscopic discoveries; (5) playing with magnets; (6) playing with the wind; (7) preparing nesting materials for birds; (8) going on expeditions; (9) corresponding with other children."[12]

Children grow and develop into healthy adults by learning in early childhood the joys, sorrows and dissappointments associated with success and failures, winning and losing, meetings and separations. I saw a boy of six and a girl of five playing together for the first time. Thirty minutes after they met, the little girl had to leave with her mother. The sadness in her eyes as she said goodbye to him was unmistakable. Later that day the little boy, in a pensive mood, was asked why he was looking so sad. His reply was "I like that little girl!" He had not forgotten the joy of making a new friend and, hours later, he was still feeling the pain of the separation. Hearing him express it confirmed the emotion I had seen in the little girl's eyes when she left. Grownups do children an injustice by ignoring or denying that they have feelings that are as real to them as to adults who assume that feelings are prerogatives of grown ups.

Adults who deny the reality of death are not able to teach children the truth about living and dying. This condition explains the confusing and misleading information that adults give to children who grieve the loss of a loved one. Telling a child who mourns that there will be a reunion with a loved one is a clear example of the adults' inability to deal with death. This is made clearer by Grollman who writes that "men are unwilling and hence unable to accept the fact that the dead are forever gone. The belief that the dead will return is born of the wish."[13] Adults can learn a lot from children's freedom to be and freedom to feel. An adult who can hold a child and cry with the child will discover a sense of wholeness probably thought to be long since gone. It can be a positive experience for the child to discover that such a human bond can exist and be shared between a child and a grown up person who almost always needs to "be strong," never to cry, to be "in control." This kind of child-adult interaction can set positive examples for children to follow. Precious moments and opportunities are lost for children and adults when intellectual reasoning precludes human to human interaction. When death occurs, children and adults should feel free to express emotions about the loss; to grieve in seclusion as well as together. Death brings good reason to cry and if not then, when? and if not, why not?

When death and dying becomes part of education and is discussed openly at school as well as in the home, what great taboo will replace it? What will be the closeted topic of the times to be overcome at some futuristic time?

Children need love, nurturing, understanding, tolerance, and relative teaching of life's complexities if they are to develop into well adjusted and total personalities. Adults who deal with children in any capacity—parents, teachers, friends and health care practitioners—need to prepare themselves to meet the challenge of providing appropriate information and support to children who cannot escape the pains of human growth and development. This includes the need to help them develop healthy attitudes toward living and dying. Given the comfort and security of love and shared feelings, children will let grown ups know their needs when they are confronted by death. For many adults this ability can be acquired through concern and deliberate effort.

Health care practitioners who deal with children must come to understand that part of their responsibility as adults is to help children to overcome ignorance and misconceptions about death. The goal of health care workers in terminal care must include interaction with the entire family. Within the family context, special effort needs to be made to encourage the children to express their thoughts and feelings about who is dying, or has died, and how they are affected by it. The importance of family members discussing their feelings about the death of a loved one promotes understanding of each individual's grief and emotional needs. Each member of the famiy grieves uniquely; each in his own way.

Open communication creates an atmosphere of acceptance. For instance, a grieving adolescent who can not talk about it may feel understood even with his inability to express deep pain. The health care worker who recognizes this may make efforts to encourage the child to talk privately. The practitioner becomes advocate to the family to help them to move along in the grief process. This service to grieving families may be made available within and without the confines of the hospital setting. Social workers, nurses, chaplains and other professionals who visit the homes of terminal patients may assist the adults with their grief and help them to be of greater help and comfort to their children.

A basic role of health care workers is to significantly touch the lives of others who reach out to us in their pain and suffering. Children suffer intensely and need sensitive persons who can support their emotional needs while teaching them to grasp the concept that suffering is an inevitable part of human living. In this way, children will be able to grow through the experience of loss. This will be easier if, as Grollman points out, one can "let the youngsters tell the adults how they feel about death, what they think, what they know, where they want to go. Respond by trying to let the youngsters know that they understand what the children are trying to say."[14]

Teaching children about death may be more effective, thus appropriate, if the adult considers the child's age, the ability of the child to comprehend, and the language one uses when explaining death to the child.

Dr. Grollman eloquently continues that "the inability of the adult to tell the young the whole truth about death, even if it were available, does not give him the prerogative to tell a lie."[15] In this sensitive area of dealing with children, one needs to be gentle. A gentle but honest approach will set the slow pace that is required. "Fear will be lessened when the discussion is focused not on the morbid details of death but on the beauty of life."[16] Since dying is part of living, sensitive adults who deal with children can help them to form a healthy perspective on life that will help to sustain them when they are confronted by death.

REFERENCES

1. Robinson, Lisa, R.N., Ph.D., *Psychological Aspects of The Care of Hospitalized Patients*, F.A. Davis, Company, Philadelphia, PA., Third Edition, 1976.
2. Bunch, Barbara and Zahra, Donna, "Dealing With Death: The Unlearned Role," *American Journal of Nursing*, Sept., 1976.

3. Grollman, Earl, *Concerning Death: A Practical Guide for the Living*, Beacon Press, Boston, 1970.
4. Stannard, David E., *The Puritan Way of Death: A Study In Religion, Culture and Social Change*, Oxford University Press, New York, 1977.
5. Redl, Fritz, *When We Deal With Children*, The Free Press, New York, Collier-MacMillan, Ltd., London, 1966.
6. Reed, Elizabeth L., *Helping Children With The Mystery of Death*, Abingdon Press, Nashville and New York, 1970.
7. Reed, Elizabeth L., *Helping Children With The Mystery of Death*, Abingdon Press, Nashville and New York, 1970.
8. Niklas, Gerald R. and Stefanics, Charlotte, *Ministry To The Hospitalized*, Paulist Press, New York, 1975.
9. Reed, Elizabeth L., *Helping Children With The Mystery of Death*, Abingdon Press, Nashville and New York, 1970.
10. Reed, Elizabeth L., *Helping Children With The Mystery of Death*, Abingdon Press, Nashville and New York, 1970.
11. Reed, Elizabeth L., *Helping Children With The Mystery of Death*, Abingdon Press, Nashville and New York, 1970.
12. Reed, Elizabeth L., *Helping Children With The Mystery of Death*, Abingdon Press, Nashville and New York, 1970.
13. Grollman, Earl, *Concerning Death: A Practical Guide for the Living*, Beacon Press, Boston, 1970.
14. Grollman, Earl, *Concerning Death: A Practical Guide for the Living*, Beacon Press, Boston, 1970.
15. Grollman, Earl, *Concerning Death: A Practical Guide for the Living*, Beacon Press, Boston, 1970.
16. Grollman, Earl, *Concerning Death: A Practical Guide for the Living*, Beacon Press, Boston, 1970.

PART IV

TERMINATION

They that love beyond the world can
not be separated by it. Death can not
kill what never dies. Nor can spirits
ever be divided, that love and live in the
same divine principle, the root and record, of their friendship......Death is
but crossing the world, as friends do
the seas; they live in one another
still....This is the comfort of friends,
that though they may be said to die, yet
their friendship and society are, in the
best sense, ever present because
immortal.[1]

—William Penn

LEARNING TO SAY GOODBYE

Think of all the people you know; or have known, who at the end of a telephone conversation, simply hang up the receiver. They never say goodbye. "Click!" All that was intended to be said has been said and, for such individuals, a goodbye is signaled by the sound of the receiver being replaced in its cradle. Thousands of people never say goodbye to anyone, whether it is a telephone encounter or face to face. Now think of yourself. Are you one of those people? If not, did you ever wonder about this style of terminating conversations? If you are one of the many people who try never to say goodbye, are you aware of it? Do you understand why you do it?

If you ask someone else why, the response is usually a mild defense: "I don't like to say goodbye;" "I hate to say goodbye;" or, still closer to the heart of the matter, "Goodbye sounds so final."

This widespread pattern of behavior in our society is probably closely linked to a subconscious, preconscious, unacknowledged fear and denial of death. It is reminiscent of the equally popular (and factual) expression that "death is such a final thing." So strong is this tendency to deny our own mortality that, not only do we resort to euphemisms to speak of death, we also employ substitute mannerisms and words to avoid and deny the use of the word (goodbye) which denotes separation (finality). For many Americans it is an established personal pattern of behavior never to say goodbye for any reason whatsoever. This evasion includes exchanges of farewells when a trip is involved, as well as at the end of an evening spent together.

Fear of death is so firmly established in our way of life in Western society that it effects us and our style of living and communicating more than we realize. Fear and superstition are among our inherited cultural traits from centuries past. Some people, for example, feel that to say "goodbye" could be bad luck. (Translated that means that to say the word could cause a final separation, presumably by death.) Phrases such as "see you tomorrow," "so long," and sometimes the unintelligible utterance of "uh-huh" followed by the "click," are all deliberate attempts to avoid acknowledging goodbye and confronting even relatively insignificant terminations in our activities of daily living. In other words, say anything, but don't say goodbye!

What is your telephone style of ending conversations? Depending on individual temperament and sense of humor, how is a "goodbye" person affected by the sudden "click" of the receiver by the "never say goodbye" person? Does it feel a bit harsh? rude? Does it negate the feeling of closure of the conversation? In almost any group there will be people who fit into both categories, either through personal habits or someone known to them. But is it a problem?

Let's first examine the word for its own meaning before going further into what it means to the people who steadfastly avoid its use. Goodbye, which is the contraction of "God be with you," is essentially a conventional expression used at parting. It is appropriate for taking leave of others either in person or at the end of a telephone conversation. Saying goodbye can give deeper meaning to the time that people have shared. It can provide the added implication that the time spent together was mutually significant. It is the same in any language: whether one says Shalom, Sayonara, Vaya Con Dios, Arrivederci, Auf Wiedersehen, or Aloha, it is a term of respect, whether in fact it is an expression of casual courtesy or deep feeling. Goodbye, simply stated, is an expression of farewell whether for the moment or forever. It frequently carries a connotation of affection! Why then does it affect so many Americans in such negative ways that efforts are deliberately made to delete it from everyday speech?

In our society, goodbye has somehow become associated with death. Saying goodbye to the dead is paradoxically acceptable to and expected by many people, but it is an expression of taboo for the living! For many people, it is easy to say goodbye to someone in whom we find disfavor, dislike or contempt. But it is never to be said to friends and loved ones "because it is a bad omen." The habit is so well established in our culture that it would require people who avoid the word to put forth conscious effort to change this idiosyncratic pattern of relating to others in meaningful relationships and casual encounters. What is the significance of this great concern about not saying goodbye? What does it matter whether or not we are able to say goodbye? Is it making the proverbial mountain out of a mole hill? Maybe not.

Is it important to learn to say goodbye? We believe it is. it is important for people in general and for people in the profession of human services. It is important because caretakers frequently find themselves in the key position of helping terminal patients and their families to work through deep emotional trauma, hopefully to the point of closure when the process of emotional and spiritual healing can begin. If it is so difficult for practitioners to say goodbye while in good health and experiencing pleasant circumstances, if health care people are unaware of the healing effects of honest expressions between patient and staff and family that make effective closure possible, how then will it be possible to say goodbye during the process of dying and at the time of death? It is of great therapeutic value to help the patient and family who can find strength and solace for having said goodbye. How can caretakers who fear expressions of goodbye be effective facilitators in terminal care, when goodbye is all that is left to share?

There are many families in America today who still "take leave of each other" in old established family traditions. They say goodbye when separating for work or school each morning; they say goodnight at bedtime and, in between, they share the day's experiences when the family is reunited each night. These old family habits from America's yester years carry certain distinct values. They facilitate mutual acknowledgements of interpersonal awareness of and individual concern for each other. They serve to further strengthen family and friendship ties and they provide a sense of value to the individuals involved. The practice is beneficial to survivors in sudden death situations. It can assuage guilt that is invariably experienced when a loved one dies unexpectedly. It helps to have at least said goodbye. It makes a difference as the waves of grief subside to recall any final and positive moments shared.

Caretakers can learn to say goodbye to terminal patients. In order to help patients and their families to reach closure by sharing goodbyes, it is logical for practitioners in health care services to begin by learning to say goodbye to each other by incorporating the term as part of their everyday language. An effective practitioner in human services does not simply turn and walk away when taking final leave of a person who is dying. At the end of a day's work or a night's tour of duty, the practitioner must take leave. Sometimes when staff members report for duty the following day, a patient they have cared for has died.

Physicians, nurses, social workers, chaplains and all other caretakers who avoid expressions of leave-taking might consider the mutually beneficial effects of acknowledging closures in day to day encounters by answering the question - What do you say when you don't say goodbye? The ability of the health care worker to say goodbye or not depends on behavior learned within the family structure. These attitudes towards separation and termination are based on early life patterning relationships within the family. For example the health care worker who grew up in a family environment where strong bonding has successfully occurred has learned certain patterns of behavior toward detaching oneself from loved ones. Such a person has learned the pain of parting, but has also learned that there is a continual interweaving of lives that will encompass his entire life. In other words, he knows that he will be experiencing the pain of separating from loved ones for the rest of his life.

Learning to let go is an important process in the individual who is open to becoming fully human. Broom and Selznick eloquently describe this phenomenon: "People as close to one another as are family members tend to acquire stable ways of dealing with each other. These may be called patterned relationships. Such patterns develop when interpretations placed on an individual's gestures in specific situations become generalized expectations for future situations.[2]

There are practitioners as well as patients and their family members who cannot express the pain of separation by verbalizing goodbyes. This includes people who find difficulty terminating any significant relationships. However, with strong staff support such attitudes can change.

Health care workers who are open and supportive of each other become aware of their attitudes towards termination. They gain insight into the cause of this behavior, grow and accept the therapeutic value of termination. This allows all involved with the dying person to move towards the acceptance of death. These are the people who are able to say goodbye at the end of a day's work and when there is full expectation that the patient will not survive the night. These are the practitioners who perceive the difficulty that families and patients experience during prolonged illness and are able to help them find the strength to say goodbye to each other. Through this supportive effort of teamwork, the family is able to make use of the present, saying and doing things for the patient and for each other as the patient moves closer to death.

When the patient has effectively completed his separation and moved into acceptance of death, when goodbyes have been expressed, he enters what Cutter describes as the last encounter. Last encounters in terminal situations are moments in the here and now when all that needs to be said has been said; when everyone involved recognizes that there will be no more forever.[3]

AUTHENTIC THERAPEUTIC ENCOUNTER WITH A DYING PERSON

In terminal care it is important that a therapeutic environment be established for the patient at the earliest possible moment following his admission to the unit. Health care workers should have the ability to move quickly into the unsettling world of the person who has been told that his condition is terminal. Hospitalization can be very traumatic for a person, especially when he suspects that he may have a terminal illness.

The moment of being told that one's condition is terminal is dreaded by most individuals. For the person admitted to hospitalization the dread is expressed in many ways. The resultant conflict between denial and hope that it is not true can be immobilizing. The person becomes immobilized because suddenly his life is threatened. Health care workers who understand the meaning of the therapeutic environment and know its value will respond to the needs of the terminal person.

The ability to transcend into the world of a dying person is the essence of authentic therapy. To be authentic is to be real, to care, to be responsive to the individual and allow him to become mutually involved on an honest level in his own care. Van Kaam supports the need of this kind of involvement. he says, "the *appeal* of a whole person can be answered only by the *presence* of a whole person. Everything that is less is a betrayal of that appeal and an escape from the giving of one's self in the authentic therapeutic encounter."[4] This relationship is a very special one which fosters trust, acceptance and enhances growth in both patient and practitioner. Kubler-Ross states, "When you're dying, if you are fortunate enough to have some prior warning (other than that we all have all the time if we come to terms with our finiteness), you get your final chance to grow, to become more truly who you really are, to become more fully human."[5] The growth that the practitioner experiences makes him more fully human through the process of sharing the mysterious core of the personality of the dying person. Van Kaam takes this thought a step further: "This unique personal core itself is an appeal to me as a full and unique human being to participate in his deepest being. I could translate this appeal into the simple words, 'please be with and for me'."[6]

The dying person's struggle to find meaning in his death may depend upon the ability of the health team to whose care he is assigned.

Eli was a 30 year old single male who was admitted to the hospital environment with a diagnosis of cancer of the lung. Further testing validated this condition and revealed matastisis to both lungs with lymph node involvement. He was assigned to the pulmonary service where the staff was accustomed to working with dying patients and their families.

The close feelings of friendship between staff and patients can emerge and develop within the confines of health care facilities the same way that relationships develop in the outside world. Many patients bring into hospitals, along with their terminal illness, the same likeable attractive human traits and personalities that draw people together anywhere else in the world. It was this way with Eli. Whenever introductions were made he quickly asked to be referred to on a first name basis. He was a person who was comfortable with himself and made others in his presence comfortable with his warmth. He was an employed electrician who had worked hard and enjoyed life right up to the day of admission to the hospital. After being told by the physician his diagnosis and prognosis, Eli mobilized himself to fight for his life. He stated to the physician that he would do all he could and was willing to comply with all that was necessary to increase his chances for survival. The physician then referred this patient to the social worker on the team and explained Eli's situation and his need for supportive treatment. When she approached him, Eli appeared to be dejected and sad. During this first encounter he expressed appreciation for staff concern but maintained an aloofness as he related what he had been told by the physician about his condition and the treatment plan. As he related his situation to the social worker, his attitude was a mixture of hope and fear, and his entire being seemed focused on survival. He was very frightened but had great hope and faith that he would be saved.

Eli realized the gravity of his situation but maintained optimism. Eli typified Roberts' thinking that "we as human beings need hope in our lives and man realizes that no matter how hopeless things may be he still maintains an element of internal hope."[7] The entire health team became involved with him in his treatment plan. The team concept for Eli's treatment regime was to establish and maintain a consistent therapeutic environment in which Eli could function at his highest possible level. During the course of his hospitalization, Eli got to know the team members as well as he openly allowed them to know him. He allowed the team to enter his world as he perceived and experienced it. He shared his hopes and his dreams and often his fantasies of what he would be doing with his life if he were still well. The team allowed him the space to deal with the feelings which he verbalized openly, and the staff listened empathetically. Staff shared each individual experience with him with each other, which allowed consistent continuity of care. This was the basis of the trust necessary for Eli to grow at his own pace.

As his condition deteriorated to the point that he moved beyond denial, making less intense expressions of hope for survival, Eli began to separate himself from the staff and significant others and to move towards his final stage of dying. However painful, the staff moved with Eli's progression toward his death. During the final days of his life the team respected his preference to share his feelings about the fact that he would not survive with one particular nurse and "his" social worker. He told these two practitioners that he had thought he would live and had tried so hard to survive, but that finally he realized that he was going to die and that it was all right. He said he was not afraid. This patient had moved to the point of finding meaning in his suffering and acceptance of his mortality.

Frankl states that "whenever one is confronted with an inescapable, unavoidable situation, whenever one has to face a fate which cannot be changed, such as an incurable disease, such as an inoperable cancer; just then one is given a last chance to actualize the highest value, to fulfill the deepest meaning, the meaning of suffering."[8]

Eli's acceptance of his impending death and his mortality further validates Frankl's statement that "what matters above all is the attitude we take toward suffering, the attitude in which we take our suffering upon ourselves."[9]

Throughout Eli's entire hospitalization, his mother maintained a constant vigil. She was an integral part of the team that gave her son (an only child) the strength and support that only a mother could give. She nurtured him by her soothing touch. She held him in her arms, whispering things inaudible to others but very special to them. She comforted him as one would a child. She was also saying goodbye to a part of herself. She opened her world of suffering to the staff, who in turn responded to her needs through nurturing and supportive treatment. During the final moments of his life the social worker who from time to time asked, "Eli, will you be here in the morning when I come to work?", finally was told by him one afternoon, "No, I'll be gone when you come back tomorrow."

The social worker met his eyes. "Are you afraid?"

"No," he responded, "I am not afraid. I know I'm going to be all right."

She talked quietly with him for awhile, and with tears streaming from her eyes they said goodbye. Eli squeezed her hand and closed his eyes. He seemed very calm. He died that night.

When all goodbyes had been said and Eli died, the staff was supportive of each other through their own individual needs in the process of grieving for a person who had become very special to them. But interwoven in their sadness was the strength and satisfaction of realizing that together and individually they had mobilized their professional skill and their human compassion and they had helped somebody to die.

All the staff involved in this patient's care emerged from the experience with the knowledge of having grown as persons who had shared in a special kind of relationship. Team members were able to say that they were irrevocably changed. They had become more aware of their own mortality, and their ability to respond to others who are facing their own deaths. This group of professional people, through this encounter, had developed a deeper understanding of each other and their own humanness. The bond that existed and sustained them was the bond in human interaction which Frankl describes in this way: "Love is the only way to grasp another human being in the innermost core of his personality. No one can become fully aware of the very essence of another human being unless he loves him."[10]

WHEN A PATIENT DIES

The mystery of death is a universal curiosity of mankind. The study of death and dying is now available through various courses offered in schools and colleges and seminars to the public. This development in America opens up the possibility of enlightenment about ourselves and our attitudes towards death. The more a human being is educated about death and the process of dying, the more accepting he will become of his own death and the mortality of others. Learning to accept death as a natural part of life is the process by which man is able to value and enjoy life. Cutter says that "knowing what you don't want somehow helps you judge how close you are to the things you do want."[11]

With changes in the American way of how we view death, part of the emerging open curiousity about death includes questions regarding life immediately after death. What happens to the person who was that body, and what happens to the body itself? Individuals are beginning to question this aspect of living and dying. This turnabout in attitudes towards death and dying in America is providing opportunities for long-suppressed, natural curiosities about human mortality to emerge. It is becoming socially acceptable to ask questions freely without fear of criticism or negative reactions from others. We are beginning to expect straight-forward opinions and, insofar as possible, to receive honest answers. How many times, for instance, have people outside the medical environment wondered about what happens when death occurs? How are relatives informed that death has occurred and by whom? What are the reactions of the family, and how are caretakers affected by the death of a patient? These and other questions may be important since the hospital deaths of patients affect many different people in various ways.

Concern for the patient's needs per se ends with the occurrence of death. Death certificates must be completed and autopsies may be requested when death is sudden or when the cause of death is unknown.

When a patient dies in the hospital a chain of events take place and are carried out strictly within set procedures. The family must be notified that the person has died. Rules and regulations vary between institutions that determine who is responsible for notifying the next of kin. Relatives are notified by telephone, telegram or in person depending on the existing circumstances. "Hospitals usually want dead bodies removed as soon as possible. If someone dies at home where others reside, there may also be a feeling of urgency to remove the body quickly from the residence. In both cases, great pressure is felt to find an undertaker at once. But how to find one, where to turn?"[12] Unless the family has made plans prior to death, selection of a funeral home may be made in a helter skelter fashion. The family is under stress and their decisions may reflect their confused state of mind. According to the editors of Consumer Reports, "only rarely is an undertaker chosen because of reasonable prices. More often than not, survivors have no idea of what the funeral negotiation will entail, what services are offered, or how prices are determined."[13] During the course of therapeutic intervention, social workers, nurses, and other health care practitioners can be of great service to families by encouraging them to plan in advance for such inevitable events, but this is a difficult task for the family to accomplish.

Because of our tendency to deny death, it almost always bears an element of what Cutter describes as "surprise to relatives, even in an aged, terminal patient."[14] This is why "no survivor can ever adequately comparative shop for these items. Yet they constitute one of the largest expenditures any family will ever have. Nowhere can a survivor find immediate, simple, and inexpensive assistance with all the practical problems he must handle."[15] Still, with effective support from a sensitive caretaker, perhaps some families will be able to try. It is worth the effort since, when death occurs, survivors who have been able to confront the realty of impeding death will experience less imposed stress if the mechanics of funeral and burial arrangements have been made in advance.

Caretakers in hospitals experience frequent encounters with death. On some services, death can be an infrequent experience, such as a sudden death on the psychiatric unit or in rehabilitation medicine. It can be a daily occurrence in Cardiac, surgical, or other Intensive Care Units. There are distinct differences in routine activities that are required in hospital deaths and those that take place when a person dies at home.

Between 1930 and 1950, hospitals gained remarkable popularity as an alternative to home care and subsequently to where patients would die. In hospitals, unlike home situations, it became the practice to "shield" the dying patient from the view of other people: the staff, the family, visitor- and other patients. Dying patients are sometimes isolated from other people and placed in private rooms. Drapes are frequently drawn around their beds on the wards; and when death occurs, roommates are occasionally engaged in conversation by staff persons to distract their attention while the body is removed from the ward. But, despite all efforts to the contrary, patients know when a death on the ward has occurred. They are aware of a difference in the usual ward routine; they over-hear conversations and they have a reliable grapevine of their own. When someone dies on a ward, other patients are affected and need the opportunity to talk with staff about the death that has occurred and to express their feelings and fears about their own situation.

In the past, when most patients died at home, the family physician was called. He examined the person for vital signs

89

and, finding none, pronounced the person dead. The funeral home was called and attendants would come and remove the body from the house in wicker baskets. The family would then be supported by the minister, neighbors and friends who had been supportive throughout the illness of the deceased. This kind of support continued for the family up to the time of the funeral and during the process of mourning. This community involvement was the custom in many areas of the United States prior to World War II. With the mobility of Americans that followed in its wake, neighborhoods gradually lost their stability. With the ultimate deaths of the neighborhood patriarchs and the constant movement of the younger surviving generations, the comfort of old established communities changed. Today no one is surprised when the big vans come to move the family next door to some distant location. It has become almost the expectation that people today move so frequently in and out of neighborhoods that the establishment of deep and long-lasting relationships are felt to be hardly worth the effort it takes to cultivate them.

Now it is seldom seen that friends and neighbors gather about the yard of a neighbor's home as the body is removed from the house, since hospital deaths are occurring today with increasing frequency. Community support for the grieving family has become remote for the average American family when death occurs, and sustained community support is no longer available. Wicker baskets for removing the dead from their homes have been replaced by more modern devices called gurneys, morgue carts and litters to remove deceased patients from the wards. The long wicker basket was a frightening, distasteful sight. The more streamlined conveyances used in hospitals today are in many ways less conspicuous (and given to more disguise) but they still evoke negative responses from some people who encounter them (enroute to the morgue) in hospital corridors and elevators. They are anxiety-provoking proof that death has occurred. The presence of death in our society stimulates discomfort in almost everyone, caretakers and laymen alike. To the physician the death of a patient can provoke feelings of defeat, humiliation, anger and helplessness. Nurses may experience very similar feelings that are compounded by the frustration that their deep investment in helping to save a person's life was insufficient. And the family, in their grief, react in unpredictable ways that range from quiet acceptance to hysteria.

In health care, workers need to anticipate and answer the families' questions openly and honestly with compassionate understanding. It is therefore the responsibility of health care workers to give support and information to grieving families. Nurses, social workers, clergymen and other health care workers can assist the bereaved in significant ways after death occurs. Families need to take care of such things as legal matters and funeral arrangements, and are often too distraught at the time of death to focus on such matters.

Staff needs to be aware especially of those individuals who have no close family members or friends available to help them. For example, an elderly couple who have for years had only themselves to care for may grow confused in dealing with the pain of loss when one of them becomes ill. They both need staff support throughout the illness and separation. When the spouse dies, the survivor needs the staff, who now become the significant others, to provide support, information and whatever assistance is needed to direct the person towards mobilizing their energy and taking charge of the pressures following death.

When a patient dies it is a time for mutual consideration for all concerned. This includes family who may be present at the time of death, survivors who arrive after death has occurred, other patients whose anxieties for their own survival are increased, and for staff who have invested so much of themselves in the care and treatment of the person who died. There needs to be a place of privacy for families to express acute grief; for staff to vent emotion and to terminate involvement with survivors as appropriate. A place of accomodation in terminal care will augment compassion and human interaction as the family is helped to deal with the difficulty of closure with staff and move into the process of griefwork that lies ahead of them. Grieving families need the appropriate setting for spontaneous cartharsis when death occurs. A staff that is sensitive to each other's needs will be in a better position to be responsive to the needs of others. In terminal care the mutual need for support, compassionate concern and consideration for patient's families and staff members alike is a never ending process.

> "In spring, when woods are getting green, I'll try and tell you what I mean:
> In summer, when the days are long, perhaps you'll understand the song:
>
> "For this must ever be
> A secret
> Kept from all the rest
> Between yourself and me."[16]
> —Lewis Carroll

LANGUAGE AS A DEFENSE MECHANISM

The difficulty of open communication about death is a learned pattern of behavior in western culture. One of the taboos about death is that you don't talk about it. Health care workers who have come to accept their own mortality have learned the value of open communication with patients and families when discussing death. Language is one of the most valuable tools in human interaction. It is the bridge for thoughts and expressions of feelings; it is how two human beings come to know each other. It is through language that we learn to share or withhold information and emotions.

James Baldwin asserts that "language, incontestably, reveals the speaker."[17] In terminal care, the caretaker needs to be aware of the language used. Baldwin further states that "people evolve a language in order to describe and thus control their circumstances, or in order not to be submerged by a reality that they cannot articulate. And, if they cannot articulate it, they are submerged."[18] Health care people communicate with and are involved with people from all walks of life, from all different cultures and from all ethnic backgrounds. They therefore would benefit by learning the language spoken and being aware of their own use of language. Dialogue between patients and practitioners, to be effective, must be meaningful and goal directed.

Open communication creates a climate for trust and comfort which allows for the honest expresson of feelings and provides opportunities for growth. As Cutter says, "The ability to talk about death does not occur naturally. It requires effort, especially if the survivor's first learning comes during, or immediately after a terminal disease."[19] It takes effort to learn how to talk about the subject of death; to be supportive to patients, to families, to staff members and with one's own family and friends. This kind of learning can best be acquired through group discussions and seminars about death that are designed to help staff get in touch with their own thoughts, feelings and attitudes about death and dying. This is necessary since death is not talked about directly and, when it must be confronted, the general tendency of most Americans is to speak of death in terms that are evasive and different from the way we use language to relate to other general topics of everyday living. The habit of subsituting euphemisms for more direct words in reference to death is so ingrained in our society that we are probably unaware of the psychological implications that our choice of words conveys. But whatever the level of our conscious awareness might be, one thing is certain: we have one language for discussing births and another for speaking of death.

A most frequent expression used with reference to death is that Mr. A "passed" this morning, or Ms. B "passed away" last night. The substitute words allow us to avoid using the more direct terms such as Mr. A died this morning, or Ms. B died last night. There is no difference in the choice of euphemisms whether referring to the death of a patient, a friend or a relative. How often have you heard someone say, for instance, that "when my cousin passed away," or "I was ten years old when my father passed." It is the exception to hear people state that the person died.

Whether the euphemism applied is passed, passed away, went away, left, went to heaven, passed on, passed on to the great beyond, or that "we lost our mother," the special terminology is widely used in our culture for several reasons. Among them is fear. Fear of death in our society is so great that we even try not to say the word death. To say that someone has "passed on" is one of the ways by which we attempt to deny that death has occurred. Passed on seems to be easier for most people to say.

Superstitious beliefs may influence our tendency to avoid using the word death. One often hears the expression that "death comes in threes." Perhaps there is fear that use of the words could be a "jinx." It seems reasonable enough since thousands of Americans "knock on wood" without hesitation for much less serious possibilities that threaten activities and circumstances of daily living. Superstition about death has prevailed from earliest history. It gained strength during the Middle Ages when preoccupation with death reached the all time high; more in fact, than during any other period in history. Present attitudes about death reflect significantly on past influences, and part of this development is reflected in our pattern of language. Cutter writes, "Regardless of what direction is taken there will be a universal need for death education; and the earlier in life, the better."[20]

Euphemisms used in reference to death are descriptive, but they only help us to deny the reality of death. This is reasonable, too, since as Cutter also asserts "denial of death's inevitablity is built into the person at an early age and it continues throughout life."[21] Close observation will reveal that, while most people will admit to being "more comfortable" with euphemisms, they may become defensive if asked why this is so. Expressions of thoughts and feelings through language becomes a problem to many people when someone dies. It is not uncommon for friends to avoid visiting families when death occurs and to explain by saying "I don't know what to say." Not knowing what to say can be embarrassing. People who relate to others quite well under pleasant situations which they would describe as being "normal" circumstances are embarrassed when confronted by death because it is distressing and uncomfortable. Cutter supports this assertion that the information is shocking, upsetting and regrettable. The initial approach to conversation is difficult but an attempt must be made to handle the painful knowledge constructively.[22]

Health care workers who are sensitive to the needs of the dying must learn to risk themselves in reaching out to the emotional needs of their patients and to the survivors. Such involvement will lessen the need to deny death. Health care workers unable to become involved on this level, due to their inability to deal with human finality, will reinforce their denial of death each time they avoid talking about death in a manner that camouflages its reality and each time they refuse to verbalize their feelings to someone who probably feels the same way. They will have lost an opportunity to grow each time they avoid mutual dialogue with a patient who dies. Such caretakers will continue to communicate with others using substitute language such as "Mr. C has expired," or "Mr. D stopped breathing." There are health care professionals who limit themselves to brief contacts with the dying or avoid them all together during the process of dying and when death occurs.

It is difficult to change early attitudes about death and dying. Practitioners who have the responsibility of caring for people who are terminal must be open to their needs so they will grow in the process. Being involved means sharing with another person, learning how he feels and his perspective about dying. To do this, open communication is vital using a language that is understood by all. Language which supports attempts to deny that death has occurred will hinder the process of necessary grief work. Grief will remain unresolved and maladaption can occur. The healthy path toward emotional recovery will be delayed.

To grow the change can be difficult, as old patterns of behavior are tenacious. It is worth the effort in confronting ourselves about death and dying and how we feel about it to learn to change our language as we learn to alter our attitudes about the normalcy of death. It will be a growth-producing experience simply to learn to say that someone has died.

REFERENCES

1. William Penn, "The Crossing," *Leaves of Gold,* edited by Clyde Francis Lytle, The Coslett Publishing Company, Wiliamsport, PA., Revised Edition, 1948.
2. Broom, Leonard and Selznick, Philip, *Sociology,* Third Edition, Harper and Row, New York, 1963.
3. Cutter, Fred, Ph.D., *Coming To Terms With Death,* Nelson and Hall Company, Chicago, 1974.
4. Van Kaam, Adrian, *On Being Yourself,* Dimension Books, Inc., New Jersey, 1972.
5. Kubler-Ross, Elisabeth, M.D., Ph.D., *Death: The Final Stage of Growth,* Prentice-Hall, Inc., 1975.
6. Van Kaam, Adrian, *Existential Foundations of Psychology,* Duquesne University Press, 1966.
7. Roberts, Sharon L., *Behavioral Concepts and The Critically Ill Patient,* Prentice-Hall, Inc., Inglewood Cliffs, N.F.

8. Frankl, Viktor E., *Psychotherapy and Existentialism,* A Clarion Book, Simon and Schuster, New York, 1967.
9. Frankl, Viktor E., *Psychotherapy and Existentialism,* A Clarion Book, Simon and Schuster, New York, 1967.
10. Frankl, Viktor E., *Psychotherapy and Existentialism,* A Clarion Book, Simon and Schuster, New York, 1967.
11. Cutter, Fred, Ph.D., *Coming To Terms With Death,* Nelson-Hall Company, New York, 1974.
12. *Funeral Consumers' Last Rights,* Editors of Consumer Reports; W.W. Norton & Co., Inc., New York, 1977.
13. *Funeral Consumers' Last Rights,* Editors of Consumer Reports; W.W. North & Co., Inc., New York, 1977.
14. Cutter, Fred E., *Coming To Terms With Death,* Nelson-Hall Company, Chicago, 1974.
15. Cutter, Fred E., *Coming To Terms With Death,* Nelson-Hall Company, Chicago, 1974.
16. Carroll, Lewis, *Alice In Wonderland;* W.W. Norton & Company, Inc., 1971.
17. Baldwin, James, "If Black English Is Not A Language, Then What Is It?" *St. Petersburg Times,* St. Petersburg, Florida, 1979.
18. Baldwin, James, "If Black English Is Not a Language, Then What Is It?" *St. Petersburg Times,* St. Petersburg, Florida, 1979.
19. Cutter, Fred E., *Coming To Terms With Death,* Nelson-Hall Company, Chicago, 1974.
20. Cutter, Fred E., *Coming To Terms With Death,* Nelson-Hall Company, Chicago, 1974.
21. Cutter, Fred E., *Coming To Terms With Death,* Nelson-Hall Company, Chicago, 1974.
22. Cutter, Fred E., *Coming To Terms With Death,* Nelson-Hall Company, Chicago, 1974.

PART V

CHANGING ATTITUDES TOWARDS TOWARDS DEATH AND DYING

CHANGING ATTITUDES WITHIN
HEALTH CARE FACILITIES

Traditional attitudes toward death and dying are changing due to developments in medical technology. Certain life
situations that were once considered fatal can now be prevented or alleviated as increased medical knowledge is dis-
seminated to the public. This knowledge informs people of
basic signs and symptoms of various forms of cancer, how to
prevent heart attacks and how to live a healthy life. Medical
research is moving ahead to find cures for catastrophic illness, implying to many people that ultimately a cure will be
found for every illness. As a result of medical science, people
in our society are enjoying a longevity that is unsurpassed by
any other period in history. This trend is leading us to believe
that there is no death. It is encouraging us to believe in our
immortality; that if death does come it will always be for
someone else. Most people feel that no matter what the
illness, through medical research a cure will be found. The
ultimate reality is that dying cannot be separated from
living.

The primary focus of health care has generally been
saving lives. To this extent the quality of life for dying people
has hardly been considered a priority goal until very recently. In the past, terminally ill patients were maintained
comfortably by keeping them clean, fed, and provided with
medication for relief of pain. There was limited communication between health care practitioners and patients
in making choices concerning their needs within the process
of dying.

Because of the upsurge in medical science and the priority of saving and extending lives, the focus now is on death
and dying as a reality and the special needs of dying people.
Accepting death as a reality has encouraged more dynamic
involvement between patients and health care practitioners.
Attitudes are changing through seminars, courses and training programs that are especially designed to enlighten
health care professionals and the general public about the
phenomen of death and dying.

Dr. Elisabeth Kubler-Ross, through her book *On Death
and Dying,* provided the public with knowledge of the stages
that dying people experience and explained what it is like to

work intimately with someone who is dying. Through this work she made the needs of the terminally ill visible. Since that time, there is a proliferation of printed material on the subject. Health care professionals now have course work included in their curricula preparing themselves to develop the skills that are required for effective intervention with people who are dying. With health care practitioners becoming more sophisticated in the care of terminal patients, health care facilities are becoming more cognizant of the needs for staff support and encouragement while working with the dying. With this comes the recognition of the need for health care facilities to also provide special ethics committees to make and to clarify policies concerning critical issues about life and death situations.

As interest in death and dying gains momentum, the increased preoccupation with the question of ethics is a natural consequence and, as an issue, our concern with ethics must be purposefully confronted. In support of the nursing profession, Dr. Mary Ellen Doona states that "good nurses have always been ethical in their practice. The great technology in health care has brought heightened awareness to each of us — that there is *more* than technology in caring for patients. The Karen Quinlans present this fact in dramatic terms."[1]

Despite the diversity of experience and knowledge that each practitioner brings to health care, each person must deal with individual concerns about ethics in this age of health technology. Dr. Doona reflects on the fact that the ethical dimension of health care is not a recent phenomenon, but that care and ethics are one. While defining ethics as a word derived from Greek, Latin and Sanskrit, meaning a system of moral principles, she says that ethical judgments of obligation determine how an individual is duty bound to act.[2] And this is the conflict that faces practitioners when these issues become confused or are unclear.

Modern health care requires that the ethics issues be resolved through a system of determined clarification for professionals who deal in the critical areas of health care practice. A committee of this nature would be the support system for everyone involved in terminal care. With clear guidelines to follow regarding such issues as "no resuscitation" and discontinuing life support orders, the nurse in charge would not be dealing with individual decisions or questions regarding a patient's life. When the health care workers are directly involved in the decision-making process of such ethical issues, they will have a clear understanding of their roles and what is expected of them in caring for a dying patient. This kind of involvement of staff could alleviate feelings of confusion and guilt. A major function of the ethics committee would be to interpret state laws regarding the right to die.

Most health care facilities are moving towards clarifying these critical issues to maintain quality care. In addition to these important changes, health care facilites are serving the community in a more generally realistic fashion. The movement today is to become one with the community in offering services to the public. An example of this is the establishment of hospice units within health care facilites and hospice liaisons with facilities that do not have their own special units for the terminally ill. Many hospitals have nurse clinical specialists and other allied professionals who work specifically with the dying patients and their families between hospital and home in addition to conducting educational programs for staff. Such activities as these support and meet staff needs.

Health care facilities that are future oriented to the problems of living and dying concern themselves with providing opportunities for practitioners to learn how to apply theoretical knowledge to practical situations in terminal care. Thus their efforts may be both professional and effective. Dr. Doona asserts that "theory is so neatly defined, while patient problems many times are chaotic."[3]

HOSPICE

The concept of hospice originated in the Middle Ages to provide comfort and care to weary travelers. It is a term which means a place of refuge, a resting palce on a journey. Hospice is a new word in the vocabulary of social workers, doctors, nurses, the clergy, allied health professionals and the general public. It is an ancient word from which the words hospital and hospitality are derived. Hospices emerged during the Crusades as comfort stations established along routes to the Holy Land, and were characterized by attitudes of caring and compassion. They offered both medical and spiritual help to travelers — many of whom were sick and dying.

During the Middle Ages, a hospice was a way station for pilgrims, generally kept by a religious order. Today, it is a way station specifically designed to maintain a meaningful, dignified quality of life for the terminally ill and their families.[4]

Hospice today has taken on new meaning. With growing public awareness and concern for terminal patients, the hospice concept has evolved into the specialized practice of providing appropriate care and treatment to dying patients. An extension of this service includes emotional support for survivors and, significantly, for staffs who provide these services. Hospice, in modern terms, is a place for travelers journeying from life to death.

The term hospice is becoming familiar as taboos toward discussion of death and dying diminish. Many people, however, are still unclear about this relatively new concept of patient care. Some people with a strong fear of death tend to harbor negative feelings toward the hospice concept by embracing outmoded attitudes and stigmas of the past. Some still question whether hospices are viewed by others as "houses of death," or whether segregation from recovering patients removes all hope of recovery for patients diagnosed as terminal. Dr. Sylvia Lack, the prime mover of Hospice in the United States and medical director of the United State's first hospice program, Hospice, Inc. of New Haven, Conn., shares the enlightened principle that a hospice is "not a place where people go to die. Rather it is a place where the dying receive the care they need to live until they die, and their families get the comfort and help they need to live with them during their illness and after their death."[5]

Most people with hospice care can and do die at home. This development is compatible with the hospice concept, which supports the humanistic value of allowing terminal patients to die at home. It is a concept that is attracting wide community support. The modern day hospice is an idea pioneered in 1967 by Dr. Cicely Saunders, a nurse, social worker and physician, at St. Christopher's Hospice in London. Hospice care is based on the special personal care that terminally ill patients require, and in many ways is different from the care given to those who will get well.

"Since more than 80% of Americans die in hospitals and nursing homes (both traditionally used for curing and convalescing), society is examining and developing places of refuge: hospices equipped to provide specialized care to patients who are emotionally preparing themselves for death,"[6] Writes John McAleenan. Terminal patients preparing for death in weeks or months need alternatives to hospitals and nursing homes which, in basic concept, are not designed to meet their total needs.

The hospice program is one way to meet the total needs of the terminally ill person with dignity and concern for the family. The emphasis of hospice care is focused on certain basic precepts such as the guidelines adopted January 26, 1978 by Hospice Care, Inc., with headquarters in Clearwater, Florida. The indicators for this facility are:

"1. Emphasis is on total care by an interdisciplinary team concerned with the physical, psychological and spiritual needs of the patient and family.
2. Medication is given not only to ease pain, but to prevent it.
3. The patient's comfort is of prime importance.
4. The family unit is involved in the treatment plan.
5. At home treatment is preferable with back-up inpatient facility available, when needed.
6. There is continuity of care, whether at home or in a facility.
7. Services are available 24 hours a day, 7 days a week.
8. Patients are accepted regardless of age, color, sex, religion, national origin or ability to pay."[7]

Similar guidelines are offered by Ryder and Ross who delineated certain hospice services based on the St. Christopher's Hospice in London, England.[8]

The goal of most hospitals and nursing homes is to rehabilitate and cure people for the purpose of their returning to daily active living, according to their level of wellness. Within a hospice concept, the goal is not to prolong life endlessly, but to insure a life fully lived, pain free, comfortable and fulfilling. This means that both the patient and the family are involved with the staff in planning the patient's care. This format is adaptable and can also be accomplished in a special unit within hospitals, and in individual nursing care facilities as well as within the individual's home. The hospice concept is one of multi-disciplinary cohesiveness. It includes physicians, nurses, social workers, clergymen, volunteers, a pharmacologist, psychiatrist, dermatologist, physical therapist and secretaries who work together as a team to insure maximum comfort and support for patients and their families.

True hospice care includes giving consideration to the emotional needs of the family during the terminal stages and at the time of death, and follow-up counseling after death occurs. Compassionate attention to the needs of the bereaved is significant since death is by far the most painful episode for the survivors to endure. The hospice, in both concept and practice, recognizes the impact of death and strives to help survivors to grieve in order to prevent maladaptions from occuring. Hospices are prepared to provide these services to patients and families because hospice staffs are trained to acknowledge, recognize and meet basic human needs in terminal care.

Terminal patients have always had to come to terms with approaching death, but traditionally they and their families have been left to their own devices without the benefits of consistent and appropriate psychological support from health care institutions. The hospice, as an alternative to traditional care, strives to prepare the patients and their families for these events and to assist the survivors in adjusting to their subsequent loss.

The hospice is more realistic and appropriate for terminal patients than the hospital, since hospice patients don't get well and hospitals are cure-oriented. Dying patients are a special-category, whether death is imminent or expected through protracted illness as in some terminal situations. The key difference in hospice is patient management based not on curing but on caring and comfort. Hospitals and nursing homes operate within a traditional orientation to patient care that is designed to provide care and treatment of convalescing patients or long term residents. Appropriate care and treatment of terminal patients requires much more in terms of specialized services and attention to their unique needs.

In terminal care there is a significant difference between task-oriented assistance and emotional support. The care and treatment of terminal patients and their families requires special attention. It must value quality and maintaining of life focus to enhance the time that is left for terminal patients to live. It is possible, in such environments, for dying patients to live fully and to share their final moments, and to maintain physical comfort and spiritual satisfaction through interaction with loved ones. Through the hospice movement, health care professionals are becoming more aware of the emotional as well as the physical needs of dying patients and are able to relate to them as total individuals with physical, emotional and spiritual needs.

As we examine and modify traditional care of terminal patients, we must continue to examine and alter traditional facilities and methods through which these services are offered. In traditional hospital setting, staff are often ill-prepared and untrained to meet the emotional needs of the dying. Within a hospice, terminal patients and families are provided with an appropriate atmosphere and an opportunity to work with well-trained and qualified staff in a setting designed to promote warmth, relaxation and individualized attention to problems. A full hospice program offers inpatient care, day care and home care. Patients who choose to die at home are able to do so with staff help and support that enables the family to manage home care and their own emotional involvement during the illness and after death occurs.

As a social worker who has served as chairman of several thanatology programs and as one who presented workshops to various health care professionals, I offer the following specific, measurable objectives and indicators for a hospice program:

1. Provision of an alternative to hospital and community nursing home care.
   INDICATOR (1) Use of a building which is ideally suited for hospice purposes through location, space-potential and design.
   (2) Adequate staff with special training in thanatology.

2. Provision of first-rate medical care, free of traditional use of heroic measures.
   INDICATOR (1) Adherence to respect for individual patient rights.
   (2) Patient participation in treatment plans.
3. Freedom from pain to allow for comfort, maintenance or achievement of an optimal level of physical, emotional, personal and social functioning.
   INDICATOR (1) Extent of use of traditional analgesics.
   (2) Extent of use of Brompton's Cocktail and/or Hospice Mixture.
4. Provision of setting that addresses itself to the unique needs of the patients.
   INDICATOR (1) Flexible visiting hours, dress codes and meal selection.
   (2) Absence of age restrictions for families and significant others.
   (3) Access to privacy, outdoor grounds and recreation.
   (4) Volunteer services for letter writing, shopping, visiting, and other appropriate services.
5. Ease family conflicts and strain while maintaining family/patient contact and participation.
   INDICATOR (1) Therapeutic milieu providing personal, family, religious and bereavement counseling.
   (2) Volunteers for legal counseling, estate planning, funeral arrangements, survivorship affiliations.
   (3) Survivors Group.
6. Reduce traditional behavioral and attitudinal manifestations associated with the care and treatment of terminal patients.
   INDICATOR (1) Education
7. Promote staff morale; reduce absenteeism and staff turnover; prevent staff burn-out.
   INDICATOR (1) Multidisciplinary team work.
   (2) Education.

(3) Therapeutic setting.
(4) Public recognition and/or financial rewards (whenever feasible).
(5) Comparison of absenteeism and staff turnover and staff burn-out with traditional health care facilities.

A hospice provides the opportunity for certain physical and emotional aspects of patient care that are not inherent in traditional health care institutions, in addition to supporting patients, families and staff. It provides space appropriate to the needs of all who use it. There should be available space in which people can work, hide, cry and find solace. There should be space for recreation, for a chapel, for children and for visitors. The hospice should be a self-contained building complete with music room, dining room and library.

This is not in any way to suggest that the hospice concept is narrowly limited to a specific building. The hospice program offers services to terminal patients and their families within the confines of their own homes. Within this concept it is possible for acute care facilities to offer (or to combine their services with) post-hospital care to terminal patients. The hallmark of a hospice program must be creativity.

As programs of care for terminal patients gain in popularity and continue to spring up throughout the united States, the need for education becomes more important; the total care concept for dying patients needs to be well understood.

Education in thanatology is of primary importance for health care practitioners and the public alike. It is unrealistic to focus on the needs of patients and families without giving concern to the needs of the care givers. Through education, staffs can learn the important aspects of emotional as well as physical care for terminal patients. At the same time, they can learn to cope with their own feelings and emotions about death and dying and the services they provide to dying patients Future health care practitioners need to learn more about themselves and their own expectations, as well as what is to be expected of them in their work with dying patients and grief-stricken families. The public can be helped to learn how to better cope with stress and the problems associated with death, the process of dying and the process of surviving significant losses.

The hospice concept includes the terminal person and his family as an active unit. The patient, however, is uniquely involved in his own death and is allowed to make certain decisions that affect his treatment. With this kind of involvement the person maintains dignity and respect as an individual by maintaining certain controls over his life. This aspect of terminal care is not common in hospitals and nursing homes.

The hospice concept is innovative as it allows for the recognition of the psychology of pain and flexibility in methods of pain control. Dr. Paul Goldfarb tells us that "pain is a great crippler. The foundation of physical care in a hospice is to get the dying person's mind off his or her body."[9] Dr. Goldfarb was probably the first doctor in the Pinellas County (Florida) area to use a pain-controlling oral mixture called "Brompton's Mixture." This medication is a combination of morphine, ethyl alcohol, cocaine, chloroform, water and flavored syrup. It is administered to patients who suffer severe cancer pain.[10]

Hospice programs are better able to meet the special needs of patients, survivors and staff than are traditional health care facilities because it is always acknowledged that care is structured for patients who are not expected to survive their illness. When death is imminent, it is important for the family unit to be together as a unique group. The hospice environment allows and supports this. It is a time for the family as a unit to involve itself in doing and saying the things that will never be done and said again. Humans share a basic need to experience valuable time together when a family member is dying. The strength of the hospice concept is its emphasis on living as fully as possible, both as an individual and as a family group, with each member having his unique feelings and thoughts that need to be shared openly in a loving receptive environment.

Family comfort does not mean the alleviation of suffering. In fact, suffering is viewed as a positive creative experience from which each unique family member is changed and grows in his own way. The main focus in hospice transcends traditional methods of care. The key word in hospice is compassion.

REFERENCES

1. Doona, Mary Ellen, R.N., Ed.D., "Ethics: Nursing's Latest Fad or Its Vitalizing Force?" Presented at Florida Nurses Association Convention, 1978.
2. Doona, Mary Ellen, R.N., Ed.D., 'Ethics: Nursing's Latest Fad or Its Vitalizing Force?" Presented at Florida Nurses Association Convention, 1978.
3. Doona, Mary Ellen, R.N., Ed.D., 'Ethics: Nursing's Latest Fad or Its Vitalizing Force?" Presented at Florida Nurses Association Convention, 1978.
4. Tozar, Eliot, "Hospices," *Practical Psychology For Physicians,* Harcourt Brace Jovanovich Publication, 1976.
5. Lack, Sylvia, M.D., Toufexis, Anastasia, "Hospice: Putting More Living Into Dying." *Hospital Tribune,* 1978.
6. McAleenan, John, *St. Petersburg Times*, St. Petersburg, Florida. 1976.
7. Elisabeth Kubler Ross, *Hospice Newsletter,* Clearwater, Florida, January 26, 1978. Vol. 1 #3.
8. Ryder, Claire F., and Ross, Diane M., "Teriminal Care: Issues and Alternatives," *Public Health Reports* Jan/Feb., 1977.
9. Goldfarb, Paul, M.D., *St. Petersburg Times,* St. Petersburg, Florida, 1977.
10. *St. Petersburg Times* article, St. Petersburg, Fla., 1977.

PART VI

GUIDELINES
FOR
THANATOLOGY PROGRAM
DEVELOPMENT

Psychologists have established that fear of failure is often the result of misleading personal comparisons. One of the most disheartening habits a person can have is to measure oneself against successful people who have become that way through years of effort in mastering their particular field. Their success is usually the result of trial and error - of not making mistakes now because they have made them before and have learned from them. They have not been afraid to fail.[1]

111

The Woods are lovely, dark and deep,
But I have promises to keep,
And miles to go before I sleep
And miles to go before I sleep.[2]
—*Robert Frost*

INTRODUCTION

The care of the terminal patient and his family within
health care agencies and in the home requires continual
support and assistance from people who are themselves prepared to cope with the stresses involved in death and dying.
The goal of modern health care in terminal illness is to meet
the complex needs of the dying and to prevent burnout in the
practitioners who are dedicated to providing these services.
This kind of professional activity is the shared responsibility
of the staff. It is the responsibility of administration to assure
that staff receives the kind of training it needs to function at
its highest level with patients who are dying. One way to
assure that practitioners gain the proper knowledge, experience and skills would be through the establishment of thanatology programs within health care facilities.

A program of this nature would have the primary goal of
training staff to deal with their own attitudes, personal fears
and feelings about death and dying. It would provide them
with greater emotional freedom to become more willing and
better prepared to offer qualitative, coordinated time and
effort to alleviating the emotional pain of dying patients and
their families. The general staff would be involved in learning to cope with the stresses of death and dying through
seminars, in-service training sessions and self-support
groups. An integral part of this activity is the multidisciplinary team approach to working with this special
group of patients.

The following Guidelines have been prepared to help
doctors, nurses, social workers, psychologists, the clergy and
all others involved in the care of terminal patients to develop
thanatology programs within their health care facilities
whether in hospitals, extended care facilities, nursing homes
or any patient care agency. Effective leadership in this ven-
ture is crucial if terminal patients are to receive the kind of
care that they need and have the right to expect. The Guidelines are specifically designed to meet the needs of any health

care agency wanting to develop a training program for its staff and are applicable to any size or complexity of health care institution. The Guidelines are basic. They are provided for staffs who:

1. recognize a felt need for staff training in death and dying.
2. feel the need for agency support in providing more effective services to patients who are dying.
3. need guidelines, encouragement and assistance in organizing training activities for staff
4. need specific help in order to work more effectively with dying patients, grieving families and with each other.
5. have viewed film strips, read books, and attended seminars; but who, wanting to develop training programs within their own settings, still find themselves asking, "where do we go from here?"

The benefits of thanatology training programs within health care institutions are that they provide support, insight and sharing of feelings and mutual problems. The result is improvement in mental health, morale and job satisfaction of members of the staff. This will enhance the opportunity to provide consistent care to patients and families during the illness, at the time of death and after death occurs.

We believe that families need support in the grief process after a significant member of the family has died. We further believe that unless the staff is nurtured in some way during the stressful activities in terminal care the true goals of compassionate care for the dying will not be fully met; staff burnout is almost inevitable under the continual pressures inherent in working with people who are dying.

Burnout is a major concern of health care practitioners. It is the professional hazard faced by those who work on a daily basis helping other people through castrophic illness and related stresses. Seymore Shubin describes burnout as a progressive phenomenon in which "you begin to dread work. You become cynical - about nursing, and you're ashamed of yourself for feeling that way. You become disgusted."[3] It is extremely important to recognize the symptoms and to discuss the problems to determine what can be done about it. As Shubin further tells us, "This progression to disillusionment or "burnout" is one of nursing's hazards; so psychologists have found. It is common among nurses, doctors, social workers, and other professionals who are so busy helping other people they neglect their own needs."[4]

One way to alleviate the problem of burnout in practitioners is through a viable thanatology program that is designed to meet the needs of staff as they help those who are dying. Open discussion of staff feelings, thoughts and fears in a multidisciplinary setting can provide a nurturing kind of strength and mutual support system that will enable staff to continue in their work with the terminally ill and their families. It is our hope that these Guidelines will be helpful in providing answers to the question, "where do we go from here?"

THE NEED FOR THANATOLOGY PROGRAMS

The need for thanatology programs within health care facilities is two-fold. It involves concerns about dying, death, grief and bereavement in terms of quality care for patients and families, as well as concerns about the health and mental well-being of the care givers.

DEFINITIONS—GOALS AND OBJECTIVES

A Thanatology Program is designed primarily to offer additional dimensions of quality care to patients and families who need help in dealing with the emotional stresses and social factors that affect their adjustment to hospitalization and terminal illness. It provides an environment within which patients and families can freely express feelings, conflicts, fears and anxieties about the terminal condition. The overall objective of such a program is to provide optimal supportive treatment; to enable patients to use their own inherent strengths; and to allow patients to retain their sense of dignity and reduce the fear of being abandoned.

A Thanatology Program is a well-planned, coordinated, multidisciplinary activity designed to offer skilled, appropriate and consistent supportive treatment to terminal patients and their families.

The primary goal of a Thanatology Program is to help patients and families communicate their feelings; to alleviate stressful and strained relationships; to provide the patient and family the opportunity to support each other, not leaving things undone and thoughts unsaid. With appropriate support of staff, patients with or without families need not die alone and lonely. Helping the dying patient and his family is an area of practice that demands the highest calibre of professional discipline and skill. It can be a gratifying experience, since in offering this help the care givers are challenged to give unselfishly of themselves.

A Thanatology Program is designed to help the staff increase its awareness and sensitivity to the needs of the dying patient and the family. This is accomplished by first helping staff to get in touch with and to deal with their own feelings and attitudes about death. The program should be available to all personnel who work in any capacity with and around terminal patients.

Hospice is a term which means a place of refuge - a resting place for travelers. It is a new word in the vocabulary of social workers, doctors, clergy and hospital staff in general and it has now taken on a new meaning. It is for "travelers" journeying from life to death. Since more than 80% of Americans now die in hospitals and nursing homes (both traditionally used for curing and convalescing), society is now examining and developing places of refuge: hospices, equipped to provide specialized care to patients who are emotionally preparing themselves for death.[5] An important extension of the hospice concept is that more patients are now able to die at home.

GENERAL PURPOSE GUIDELINES

Practitioners and research investigators in recent years have become intensely interested in the previously neglected subject of death and dying. Thanks to the efforts of Dr. Elisabeth Kubler-Ross, the subject of death is no longer taboo. We have moved from mere discussion to seeking methods of answering the question of what constitutes excellent care for the terminally ill patient. Unless we establish explicit standards of care for the terminally ill, there will be fragmented efforts and lack of coordination among nurses, doctors, social workers, medical specialists, psychologists, psychiatrists and all other well-meaning members of hospital staffs. Unless there is appropriate and consistent support offered by a coordinated staff, patients and families trying to deal with their stresses will fall between "specialists" with a resultant absence of qualitative emotional support.

Many terminal patients in health care facilities and their families are not receiving consistent, appropriate emotional support. Many staff members have not had the opportunity to learn how to cope with the stresses of death and dying.

In some health care facilities, efforts to educate staff in thanatology are fragmented. Some of the problems are due to lack of structure and no clear lines of responsibility for continuity of a program. If, for instance, the significant leader of this effort becomes ill or leaves, there is usually no replacement and the program ceases to exist.

These Guidelines can serve as a unifying content core for the assessment, planning, organizing and implementing of thanatology programs in any health care agency that is geared to meet the special needs of dying patients and their families.

These Guidelines are designed to provide direction for care takers who have a vested interest in learning how to develop the skills required for helping patients during various phases of terminal illness, assisting families, and organizing a viable program to insure that terminal patients have the opportunity to express themselves. A well-coordinated program can insure improved emotional treatment of the terminal patient and the family. It can also serve as a means of increasing staff morale. The experienced practitioner is in an excellent position to respond to the challenges and to make significant contributions to patients, families and staff.

Guidelines of Care

Throughout this book the terms patients, families and staff are frequently used together. This is to emphasize the fact that unless equal significance is given to the needs of the family and the staff who provide terminal services, the approach to developing a comprehensive thanatology program is unrealistic. Guidelines of care established ensure continuity of care for terminal patients. This requires a combination of guidelines for patients, guidelines for family and guidelines for staff.

117

We are not suggesting that working closely with terminal patients and their families is an easy task. To the contrary, it is often difficult; a great challenge which can be emotionally draining. It can also be highly rewarding, providing that the staff is sufficiently motivated, trained and supported in the process. Without these ingredients, certain staff members will not be able to provide appropriate care to terminal patients and families despite the need.

We believe guidelines are necessary to promote mutual support and understanding among staff. It is necessary to insure quality care for the terminally ill. It would, at the same time, provide compassion and concern for family and significant others.

Burnout results from staff who are often alone and frustrated when giving care to the terminally ill, while having no specific set of guidelines to direct them.

Guidelines For Patients

Since each patient is a unique person with individual needs, the rules and regulations concerning their care and treatment must be flexible. The holistic concept of care requires that each individual be cared for according to needs presented. No patient should be abandoned in receiving medical or nursing intervention despite the nearness of death. To live until one dies and to be able to do it comfortably and with dignity should be a treatment goal of the staff. No terminal patient should be allowed to suffer unnecessarily. In the process of dying all efforts should be made to maintain the person's dignity and morale.

The patient's wishes governing his care should be considered. Those who choose to forego extraordinary means to prolong life within reasonable means deserve to be heard. This is dependent on the legal system in operation in each state including the responsibilities and legal rights of the family, as well as the health care providers.

A guideline to promote a feeling of safety and security for terminal patients would enhance a peaceful death, knowing he will not be alone as death draws near. The patient is not deprived during the final experience of life. In an atmosphere of open communication, the patient feels comfortable knowing that his needs will be met.

Consideration for visitation in the hospital environment should be permitted for everyone special to the patient, despite age or gender. If the patient desires privacy with a loved one, his wish should be respected and accommodated.

In some private institutions, special rooms are set aside where the dying person lives in a more homelike atmosphere. The staff understand and value the time that the patient is able to share in meaningful ways with loved ones, knowing that time is of the essence for the terminally ill.

Guidelines For Family

Open communication between the family and staff is necessary to meet the emotional needs of the family. Family members are experiencing a major change due to the impending loss. Staff can be helpful and supportive in meeting these needs by being available to answer questions and clarify issues concerning the patient. In some families, the loss of a loved one can be overwhelming to the point of causing dysfunction within the family unit. Staff that are considerate and compassionate can help the family grow from the painful experience; help each other and the dying patient. Conflicts that arise within the family can be resolved through purposeful and meaningful therapeutic interaction with staff.

Families can be helped to learn to say good-bye. The opportunity to experience closure, to say what needs to be said for the last time can not be overestimated in terms of future value for the survivors. At the time of death, the terminal patient's work is finished. The work of the survivors has just begun.

Guidelines For Staff

All staff who work with terminal patients need to know how to meet the needs of the dying. Interpersonal relationships between patients and staff are necessary to maintain continuity of care.

A team spirit of respect and caring about each other is the most effective method of helping one another to deal with the inherent stresses of working with dying patients and distraught families. Staff members need to feel safe expressing their feelings openly, and comfortable helping each other. A sense of security within this environment can develop and provide emotional support for every member of the team. Growth is enhanced when there is love and compassion among staff.

DEVELOPMENT OF A
THANATOLOGY PROGRAM
General Responsibilities

Health-care professionals, with their knowledge of human behavior, patient advocacy and emphasis placed on alleviation of emotional pain and suffering, are in an excellent position to promote qualitative services for terminal patients and families caught up in the crisis of one of life's most difficult situations. The task will be easier as they come to realize that the process of dying is a dynamic phase of living, rather than an end in itself. There are stages of dying and, in this process, stages of surviving. Health care professionals have the responsibility of reaching toward people to meet their needs. There is no substitute for the human element in deep emotional situations.

There is a vast increase in community resources available to families of terminal patients. Widow-to-Widow is gaining in popularity as a grief-support group; less popular but just as needed are its counterparts, Widower-to-Widower and Parent-to-Parent. It is a positive development that we are coming to recognize the fact that men who grieve also need support from others. These and other such peer groups offer immediate support systems for follow-up care and are especially helpful and therapeutic for high-risk survivors. The American Cancer Society offers many services to terminal patients and families including transportation, speech therapy, financial assistance in securing home care, hospital equipment, dressings, assistance with special needs, rehabilitation services through the Volunteer Visitor Program and numerous other miscellaneous services. Through knowledge of community resources and community potential, care givers are in a unique position to provide information and referrals to patients and families when the need arises for help outside an institutional setting.

Terminal patients sometimes ask to be allowed to go

home to die. Such patients, having lived with loved ones and around friends in familiar surroundings, want to return to the warmth, privacy and emotional security of their homes for shared grief and mutual support. This is sometimes possible if the family is willing and able to care for the patient at home. In addition to medical considerations, there must be a qualitative assessment and plan for hospital support. The family must be allowed to express freely their feelings about the responsibility and fears involved in home care of a terminal patient. More terminal patients could go home to die if provided with supervised care. The team assessment is very important in this area of patient care. To be mutually beneficial, home care for terminal patients must reflect individual family life-styles and the established quality of patient/family relationships. This emphasizes the need for increasing the involvement and utilization of appropriate community resources in order to focus on the holistic approach to helping patients and families.

There is a special responsibility to terminal patients who die in health care agencies who have no one other than the staff to depend upon. In such situations, a staff member should be available to sit, listen and talk with the patient with regularity; even short intervals are therapeutic for many patients. It is important to get to know patients as well as possible in order to recognize and properly respond to their moods, attitudes and cues.

Terminal patients struggle with problems common to all other patients whose lives have been emotionally, socially, and financially disrupted by serious illness. Recognition of the significance of helping them and their families to clarify, plan and resolve these related problems provides the opportunity for better patient responsiveness to treatment and adjustment to hospitalization. It allows for improved family interaction and frees them to deal more effectively with the effects of their changing lives through mutual support systems.

Recognition of and respect for the feelings of staff and the emotional drain imposed on them from working closely with the dying patient can promote a climate for mutual trust, support, planning and decision making by the health team members.

With clearer understanding of self and awareness of

what the patient may experience during terminal illness and how he may try to cope, the care giver who knows him best can help staff to understand the effects of his illness upon him and his family. The care giver then contributes significantly to staff ability to relate helpfully to the patient and his family during the terminal stages, and to the family at the time of the patient's death.

Active participation by the multidisciplinary team in the assessment and planning for patients in the program supports the medical determination that the patient is terminal and can benefit from psycho-social supportive treatment as an extension of the medical treatment plan. The team contributes significantly through provision of evaluative information and knowledge of the patient's personal, social and economic situation as it relates to family, financial and emotional problems caused by his illness.

Administrative Responsibilities

The professional practitioner functions within the framework of agency policy and is accountable for providing quality care to its patients. This, therefore, aligns care givers with achieving the agency's total policy which is to provide the highest level of care to the maximum number of patients.

A multidisciplinary team effort has definite responsibilities in the planning, development and advancement of a qualitative, effective Thanatology Program. A built-in design is the essential ingredient of collaboration with colleagues in other disciplines.

In order to assure unity of purpose there is the need for cooperation and coordinated efforts in the planning, development and administration of the program and its services.

Clear perspective and understanding of the goals between disciplines begins with education. It is established through the experiences and satisfactions derived from concerted efforts to comfort and assist terminal patients. There is much to be learned and education of professional staff is necessary to overcome attitudes and myths that hamper progress.

In keeping with fundamental policies that may be established by the health care agency, a primary administrative responsibility lies in the basic planning of a thanatology program appropriate for multi-disciplinary team functioning. It is a continuous process and must be revised with flexibility according to changing needs and circumstances.

The health team has a key responsibility and role in influencing the general environment in which patients will receive these services. It must assume increasing responsibility and active participation in the program promotion and decision-making process. A major role is that of patient advocacy. This involves interpretation and intermediary activities to bridge the gaps between bureaucracy and individuals, patients and families, as well as the social and clinical environment.

Organization of plans includes keeping administration apprised and involved in the process. Consulting administrative staff is helpful in determining basic administrative guidelines, defining and clarifying specific assignments or reassignments. It is of vital importance that the channels of communication between administration and the health team remain open.

Resources must be determined and assembled in terms of space, time, personnel and other related variables to assure that the program can be carried out making maximum use of time and purpose.

The Role of the Coordinator

These guidelines include administrative aspects and principles of program development to further assist the practitioner who assumes the role of program coordinator. The purpose is to encourage, promote and extend the scope of the thanatology program as an educational and practical service to terminal patients, families and staff.

A coordinator is desirable and necessary since such an effort requires leadership to establish, promote and maintain a full-time comprehensive program.

The coordinator position will serve as a motivating factor for interested practitioners to avail themselves of the opportunities for personal and professional growth; to learn, to study, to consult, to research and develop the skills required to administer a program which is gaining in need and popularity.

123

Appropriate duties of a thanatology program coordinator at a professional level include aspects of all major administrative components including planning, organizing, directing, coordinating and controlling. It requires personal and professional commitment.

The coordinator will:

(1) formulate program goals;
(2) legitimize the recognized need for the program;
(3) provide a vehicle for program continuity;
(4) provide and establish a significant contribution to improve quality patient care;
(5) set an example in health-care techniques for society and other health-care facilities to emulate;
(6) develop, promote and guide a thanatology program that is comprehensive and available to university students from a multidisciplinary academic background who are interested in preparing and developing their capabilities for entering careers in this area of health care;
(7) identify areas of the program that are conducive to research and coordinate the health care agency with university interests and student training;
(8) have administrative skills, established qualifications and experience in terminal care. The coordinator should have genuine interest and concern for helping patients and families as well as having the ability to communicate with skill and confidence of purpose. Other factors include having the ability to collaborate and to work comfortably and effectively with a multidisciplinary health team.

The coordinator further provides direct services to terminal patients, families and significant others through coordinated activities of a multidisciplinary team; develops and carries out program plans in coordination with other services; participates in community planning for development of health-related and other appropriate resources for terminal patients and their families; establishes and maintains effective working relationships with local agencies concerned with the special needs of terminal patients such as American Red Cross and Hospice Programs; evaluates the progress of the unit teams and the needs for further program development through regular meetings with the thanatology committee; and plans with community efforts in developing seminars and workshops on subjects pertaining to death and dying.

These Guidelines provide clinical, professional and administrative principles and procedures to enable the coordinator to develop and manage a thanatology program. This includes collaboration with the medical/nursing staff and other related disciplines to explore and promote unity and cooperation to initiate a program.

The coordinator may be representative of any health care discipline.

The Thanatology Program Committee: Purpose, Function and Membership Selection

A thanatology committee in any large metropolitan or university hospital could follow these Guidelines with little or no difficulty. Small health care agencies will find these Guidelines to be adaptable to suit their individual needs and circumstances. The committee is established by the coordinator from various disciplines for the purpose of determining program goals. It includes three basic functions: (1) to develop a program; (2) to teach staff; and (3) to evaluate the program for outcome. The major purpose of the committee is to designate and apply its membership responsibilities and function to the Thanatology Program. Specifically the committee is expected to:

1. Develop and determine specific principles and methods for program educational and training series on an ongoing basis.
2. Develop a comprehensive Thanatology Training Program designed to teach multidisciplinary staff fundamental and advanced skills and techniques of working more effectively with terminal patients and their families.
3. Establish a climate for mutual support, planning and decision making for the health team members;
4. Serve as identifiable, available resource personnel to staff in a supportive and informative manner to alleviate stresses imposed by working with terminal patients and to further promote spirit of concern, trust and the concept of teamwork.

5. Develop and organize training resources to include local/national speakers, films, videotapes, in-service training sessions, adequate literary materials through agency and public libraries, bibliographies, and so on.
6. Involve participation of patients, families and significant others as appropriate in training sessions that will be mutually beneficial, cathartic, learning experiences.
7. Develop a course outline for each training series; modify as indicated according to staff needs and interests.
8. Provide certificates for course completion to participants who meet course requirements as determined by the committee.
9. Develop a climate for creative team functioning in assisting terminal patients and families.
10. Establish involvement with the community to promote cooperative services to patients and families and to establish additional resourses.
11. Arrange for tape recording and videotaping of pre-selected sessions to be used as resources for future training series if desirable.
12. Help staff understand what the patient may experience during terminal phases and how the patient may try to cope.
13. Help staff understand the effects of the patient's dying (and death) upon family members and signifciant others; how they may try to cope; and the effects on other patients when death occurs.
14. Contribute to staff's ability to relate helpfully and more comfortably to the patient and family during the dying process and to the family at the time of the patient's death.
15. Promote staff awareness of:
    a. feelings which can be triggered within the staff, and the emotional drain imposed on them when working with dying patients and grieving families.
    b. the need to determine, explain and encourage effective, appropriate coping mechanisms for dealing with stress.
    c. Train selected staff members to function as "unit teams" who would be available to terminal patients and family on a consistent basis.

The need for a thanatology unit team is based on the premise that not all staff are sufficiently capable of or inclined to work with terminal patients beyond the traditionally required scope of service. It is for this percentage of reluctant staff that general training and educational opportunities are provided in the hope that they might benefit through secondary gains including increased morale. The general staff, therefore, would be involved in learning to cope with death and dying through seminars, training sessions and by example.

It is a function of the committee to participate in the selection of the unit team members from the training participants in order to establish unit teams comprised of the most highly interested, motivated, and capable practitioners.

It is the responsibility of the committee to provide support, counsel and guidance to unit teams on an as-needed basis.

A significant program contribution of the committee may be the establishment of a reference library.

Membership Selection

Thanatology Program Committee members should be selected with certain prerequisites:

(1) membership must be multidisciplinary;
(2) each member must have a vested belief in the program philosophy and goals with a sincere interest in the promotion and accountability for positive outcome through united efforts to achieve common goals.

Selection of a particular unit or service for a pilot program should be based on a ratio of occurring deaths and interest of the unit/service personnel.

The time frame for conducting staff training series needs to be flexible.

In instances where the demands of units or services preclude a significant number of participants attending the same consecutive sessions at the same time, or absences due to change of shifts, it is suggested that a series of concurrent sessions can be conducted using the same course outline to insure continuity of content and participation. For instance, a 6-week series conducted on Tuesday and Wednesday, same time, same content, same service, will allow for greater staff participation. This is only a suggestion, however, as each Committee has the flexibility and responsibility to resolve unique problems according to individual agency needs and situations.

While printed materials and audio-visual aids are helpful resources and may be utilized to augment learning experiences, verbal communication is the key to enabling staff to "open up," express and share feelings, thereby gaining maximal benefit from the program. Films used in training may complement verbal exchange rather than serve as a teaching method in and of itself. The Committee should preview and select ahead of time any film to be used in training sessions. Films, however, should not be used in lieu of verbal communication.

The Committee should evaluate and modify the program through on-going processes of evaluation during and at the end of each training series, and prior to the beginning of a new series.

Sample Pretest

PRETEST FOR THANATOLOGY TRAINING PROGRAM

Self-evaluation of learning needs before training activities

List at least three to five things you feel the need to know and hope to learn about death and dying in relation to your work.

1. _____

   _____

2. _____

   _____

3. _____

_____

4. _____

_____

5. _____

_____

Sample Questionnaire

EVALUATION OF THANATOLOGY TRAINING COURSE. Your frank observations will be of great help in planning future sessions and in presenting them as effectively as possible. With this in mind, will you please answer the following questions? You need not sign your name.

1. On a scale of 1 to 10, how would you rate the value of this training course in meeting your needs in terminal care?   1 2 3 4 5 6 7 8 9 10
2. If audio-visual aids were used, of what value were they to you?   1 2 3 4 5 6 7 8 9 10
3. The course ( )was ( )was not repetitive of information and materials I had already known and/or used.
4. The course ( )was ( )was not worth the time I spent in attendance.
5. Was this course on death and dying beneficial to your growth and development in your present assignment? ( )yes   ( )no   ( )somewhat
6. The material covered in this course ( )was ( )was not relevant to my job situation.
7. As a result of this course, ( )I am ( )I am not better able to define my own role and goals regarding terminal care practices at the place of my employment.

8. What do you consider the most significant strengths of this course as presented?

_____

_____

9. What do you consider the most significant weaknesses of this course as presented?

_____

_____

10. How effective were the committee members in meeting your training needs? _____

11. On a scale of 1 to 10, how would you rate the committee members:

Knowledge of subject matter 1 2 3 4 5 6 7 8 9 10

Planning & presenation of subject
  matter 1 2 3 4 5 6 7 8 9 10

Skill in communicating thoughts
  & ideas to others 1 2 3 4 5 6 7 8 9 10

Sensitivity to the group and individual
  needs in this emotional subject 1 2 3 4 5 6 7 8 9 10

12. Which of the activities were not helpful to you in terms of meeting your learning needs?

_____

_____

13. Would you add/delete anything in future courses?
    Explain — _____

_____

14. How might this course be improved? _____

IMPLEMENTING THE PROGRAM

Patient Referral to the Program

Application of a multidisciplinary approach to terminal patient care contributes significantly to the total-care plan as it provides close contact with patient, family and staff. A high degree of coordination and collaboration with unit staff and other services is necessary in order to assure that all aspects of the patient's needs influence the plans for comprehensive treatment. For participation in the program, terminal patients and families may be referred for this specialized service through several methods and considerations:

1. Terminal patients and families will be referred by self, social workers, unit physicians, nurses or any significant others such as friends and relatives.
2. Appropriate referrals should include patients who are newly admitted and diagnosed as terminal. This would include patients with terminal diagnoses whether or not there is evidence of mental stress.
3. Patients should be referred as soon as possible after diagnoses to allow opportunity and sufficient time to benefit from the program.
4. Patients diagnosed as terminal should be referred whether or not they have been informed of their terminal condition. While it is the responsibility of the physician to inform the patient that he is terminal, it is the responsibility of the health care team to assist all patients. The initial approach is the same as for any patient: simply to offer service and be available.
5. It is the responsibility of the thanatology unit team to communicate with physicians to determine which patients have or have not been informed of their terminal states.
6. Program goals should be appropriately and clearly explained to patients and their families who are referred to the program.
7. Patients and their families reserve the right to accept or reject program participation. The option should remain open to them.

Objectives and Guidelines for Unit Teams

1. The team will be multidisciplinary.
2. The team will be aware of each terminal patient and family on the unit.
3. The team will conduct unit conferences to assess the needs of terminal patients and establish goals for working with each patient and family.
4. Plans will be entered on the Nursing Care Plan and activities charted in patient's medical record.
5. There will be communication between the unit staff and the program coordinator reporting progress, problems and making recommendations.

6. The team should be accessible to each other for support, consultation and ventilation of feelings.
7. Unit teams may become autonomous during the process of training depending more on their own resources and less on the committee except for meeting specific needs and participating in refresher in-service programs.
8. Each team will serve as a viable program nucleus on individual units.
9. Unit teams will include but not be limited to: head nurse or designee, physician, social worker, dietician, chaplain, psychologist or any other member of the health team on the unit.

Suggested Topics for Discussion and Use in Training Series: Myths About Terminal Patients

Death is an appropriate part of living. As difficult as it is for most of us to accept this concept it is important that we confront it. The major barriers to effective terminal care are our attitudes and beliefs. Fear and myths about death and dying are part of the attitudes that inhibit our ability to enter the world of the dying person as he is experiencing it. For these reasons the following myths offered by Weisman could provoke further discussion among health care practitioners who seek answers for themselves regarding working with people who are dying.

1. Only suicidal and psychotic people are willing to die. Even when death is inevitable, no one wants to die.
2. Fear of death is the most natural and basic fear of man. The closer he comes to death, the more intense the fear becomes.
3. Reconciliation with death and preparation for death are impossible. Therefore, say as little as possible to dying people; turn their questions aside; and use any means to deny, dissimulate and avoid open confrontation.
4. Dying people do not really want to know what the

future holds. Otherwise, they would ask more questions. To force a discussion or to insist upon unwelcome information is risky. The patient might lose all hope. He might commit suicide, become very depressed or even die more quickly.

5. After speaking with family members, the doctor should treat the patient as long as possible. Then, when further benefit seems unlikely the patient should be left alone, except for relieving pain. He will then withdraw and die in peace, without further anguish or disturbance.

6. It is reckless, if not cruel, to inflict unnecessary suffering upon the patient or his family. The patient is doomed; nothing can really make any difference. Survivors should accept the futility, but realize they will get over the loss.

7. Physicians can deal with all phases of the dying process because of their scientific training and clinical experience. The emotional and psychological sides of dying are vastly over-emphasized. Consultation with social workers, psychologists and psychiatrists is unnecessary. The clergy might be called upon, but only when death is near. The doctor has no further obligation after the patient's death.[6]

Myths about death and dying are age-old and varied; they are not easily dispelled. Myths reinforce and tend to perpetuate themselves. For example, there are people who maintain that if all patients had made their peace with God there would be no need for thanatology programs. It is the "touching" of a person who is in emotional pain by another person who recognizes, understands and cares that brings relief and mutual satisfaction into a therapeutic relationship. Touching in this sense means the ability to perceive the suffering of another human being. It means being able to empathize with the person, and to respond appropriately and effectively at the right time.

Being a patient in a hospital can be a traumatic experience even for people who are admitted for care knowing that their stay will be brief and that their illness is not viewed as life-threatening. The emotional trauma that people with catastrophic disease experience is much greater.

Terminal patients are frightened people. They feel insecure in unfamiliar surroundings. They fear the worst, having limited information about their situation and fear of what yet lies ahead for them. Hospital confinement is impersonal, with things constantly being done to them and for them. They are no longer in control of their lives. They would rather be at home, or at work, but they are now patients; they are no longer people with independent lives. They have, by necessity, become dependent upon others for help. Terminal care involves working with the elderly, middle-aged, young, alert, or confused patient as well as others who are comatose or acutely ill. Discuss appropriate therapeutic intervention:

Approaches to working with
Terminal Patients

1. In what ways are people affected as individuals when they become hospital patients?
2. How are families affected when a family member is hospitalized for a serious illness?
3. What can staff do to help a newly admitted patient adjust to hospitalization?
4. What is implied by the statement that "hospital care needs to become more humanized?"
5. What do caretakers need to become better prepared to work effectively with terminal patients?
6. Is it necessary for staff to know a terminal patient for a long time in order to be emotionally supportive?
7. How do your own feelings determine the manner in which you might respond to a terminal patient who is angry?
8. How would you handle a patient who is denying the seriousness of his illness?
9. What would your response be if the patient told you he would be up and back to work in a week or so and you know that he is terminal?
10. What would you say if a patient said "I'm going to eat everything they give me because I know it's the only way I'm ever going to beat this thing."
11. What would you do if a male patient started to cry when you asked if you could help him?
12. How would you respond to a female patient who began to cry when you asked if you could help her?

13. How would you feel when any patient you were working with started to cry?
14. How would you respond to a patient who said, "I thought I was going to make it when I came in here, but I know now this will be the last Thanksgiving I'll ever see?"
15. How do terminal patients bargain for life?
    a) Did you ever bargain for anything? Explain.
    b) How did you feel if you did not get what you bargained for?
16. Have you ever lost something of value that caused you to grieve?
17. There is a time to be actively supportive in terminal care and a time to be supportive in passive ways. What does this statement mean? Explain the difference between active and passive support; give examples of each.
18. How do caretakers know what to say to someone who is dying?
19. What makes a patient more responsive to one person than to another?
20. What do terminal patients think about?
21. What do terminal patients talk about?
22. What do they want from staff?
23. Most people want to live. Does that mean that it is impossible to experience acceptance of death?
24. Do you feel that patients who have family support have no need of supportive intervention from staff?
25. Do you believe that all terminal patients seek religious counseling before they die whether they are religious, atheistic or agnostic?
26. Are most patients, when informed that their illness is terminal, likely to give up all hope and lose the will to live?
27. Do you believe that most patients would prefer not to be informed of their terminal conditions?
28. Would you prefer not to be told if you had a terminal disease? Explain.
29. What are some of the things a terminal patient might ask you that would make you feel uncomfortable? Name at least three.
30. If you decide to work at taking a positive attitude toward death, what would you be trying to accomplish and how would you go about it?

31. If you offered your services to a terminal patient and the patient asked "but how can you help me? I am going to die," what would you say?
32. You are a social worker in a medical setting. What is your therapeutic role in terminal care?
33. You are a nurse in a hospital setting. What is your therapeutic role with patients who are dying?
34. What are the inter-related roles of the nurse and the social worker in the care and treatment of terminal patients? In what ways are they (1) different, (2) similar, (3) the same? Explain.
35. In what ways does terminal care differ from regular patient care?
36. What do you hope to contribute to quality terminal care?
37. What do you hope to learn from studying thanatology?
38. How does religion influence a person's attitude toward death?
39. How does religion influence a person's attitude toward life?
40. What are your feelings about patients who refuse to eat or to take treatment in order to hasten death?
41. How effectively can a health care provider who is afraid of dying patients function in a medical setting?
42. What is the difference between fear of death and fear of dying?
43. Describe the visceral feelings you usually experience while discussing death.
44. Why is it more difficult for some people to talk about death than it is for others?
45. What is the difference between internalizing and intellectualizing in the study of death and dying?
46. What is the meaning of the term "staff burn-out" in terminal care?
47. Why do some people who work in terminal care on a regular basis tend to develop stoic attitudes toward dying patients?
48. Does being professional mean that you must show no emotion?
49. Where emotions are concerned, what is the difference between being strong and being in control?
50. Why do some people feel a greater need than others to "be strong?"

51. What symptoms indicate that the family is experiencing great stress?
52. How can a health care worker help a grieving family?
53. What is the significant difference between listening and hearing?
54. Name several ways in which a grieving family might be affected by a protracted illness?
55. How should terminal illness and death be discussed with children? Explain.
56. How would you intervene with parents grieving the impending death of their child?
57. How would you support and comfort a child who is dying?
58. How do you learn what death or dying means to a child?
59. In what ways can staff who work with dying children support each other?
60. A dying child may reflect the attitudes of the people around him. (Discuss)
61. If families do not ask for help, how can staff become aware of their needs?
62. Does a terminal illness of a relative necessarily result in closer relationships within the family unit?
63. Should staff permit families to assist in the patient's care? Explain.
64. Why do some relatives have a need to assist in the physical care of terminal patients?
65. What is the value of having knowledge of cultural/ethnic backgrounds of families?
66. How does the statement, "hearing is the last to go," relate to terminal care for comatose patients?

ROLE PLAYING

Fear is the most basic of all reasons that people feel so helpless in the presence of death and in the care of dying patients. During seminars or thanatology training programs, when participants are asked to express a physical feeling during a particular moment in discussing death, among the most frequent responses is, "I feel a tight knot in my stomach." If the person is willing to further describe the feeling, it is usually expressed as "fear," "scared of dying," "scared to die," or an occasional declaration of "I don't want to die!"

Once the fear of death is acknowledged, the feeling of helplessness in working with dying patients will diminish. It is at this point that the practitioner can begin to accept the challenge to become more supportive to terminal patients and families. Each terminal patient is a unique individual and requires a unique plan of treatment tailored to meet his individual needs. Staff members, like patients, are at different stages in dealing with their own feelings about death and the process of dying. Since fear seems to be the basis for negative attitudes toward death and dying, it is fear which needs to be confronted and, to the best of one's ability, understood. Several approaches can be utilized in the process of accomplishing this task.

Exercise One

1. Participants form a circle of chairs and, if possible, there should be sufficient space between the chairs to give each individual a personal feeling of aloneness.
2. One person in the group should make a list of the words used by participants to express their feelings about death (i.e. sad, angry, and so on).
3. The group leader (or instructor) should have available a heavy book and the "name" of the book is "Death."
4. The leader passes the book to the person to the left and makes the following statement: "This book is death. Embrace it and tell us how you feel about it."
5. The book is passed from one participant to the other in this manner until each person has held it and expressed his/her feelings.
6. The book is then passed to the leader who expresses feelings as the others have done.
7. The group then discusses feelings, observations and the expressions noted on the list and how they relate to their work in terminal care.

    The purposes of this exercise are: (1) to provide participants the opportunity to discover insight and to acknowledge to peers their own gut-level feelings about death and what it means to them as individuals; (2) to examine the willingness and ability of participants (coworkers) to share personal feelings associated with death and dying; and (3) to encourage communication and peer support. A certain amount of intellectualizing can be expected and the exercise may be awkward when first attempted. There can be feelings of embarrassment for people who are unaccustomed to sharing their feelings with anyone in an open and honest fashion, especially with strangers. Consideration must be given to participants who choose not to share their feelings, for those who deny experiencing any feelings at all, and for those who choose not to participate.

The purpose of this or any such exercise in this book is not to intimidate or to force anyone to express feelings or emotions they might prefer not to risk or to share. It should be respected that each individual grows and develops at his own pace. Risking any part of one's self requires trust. This exercise is offered with several other goals in mind. It is self-revealing in terms of basic fears associated with death and dying; it can help to facilitate mutual respect, consideration and trust of staff in a therapeutic setting; it helps staff to learn to communicate, and to share feelings about death and dying; it encourages discussion about terminal patients and families among people who work and study in the same situations and circumstances. It is designed to help facilitate insight into how one feels about one's own mortality and how such feelings are reflected in the kind of care provided to dying patients. Once these basic problems are confronted, methods can be determned for resolving them as much as possible.

Before engaging in this exercise or any other contained here, we feel it necessary to express the need for each participant to be aware that, almost without exception, one or more members of the group will be in the process of coping with the pain of acute or unresolved grief in varying degrees of intensity. Insofar as possible, it is suggested that this exercise be approached with appreciation for the possibility of known and unknown distressful factors in the personal lives of all participants.

Exercise Two

Let's assume this is the first terminal patient that this recent graduate social worker has ever seen; that the social worker has never before talked with anyone who is in the process of dying. What is the social worker expected to do? to say? How will the patient respond? The young social worker feels uncomfortable and scared and wonders: What does a person say to someone who is dying? What will I say? How will the patient react? What if he wants to talk about the fact that he is going to die? What will I say? It scares me too that he is only thirty-six and he's dying!

The immediate feeling of the social worker might logically be dread of the assignment; fear of facing someone who is dying; bewilderment and self-pity for feeling inadequate to meet the challenge, anger at the physician for referring the patient in the first place and a final resolve to get it over as quickly as possible. In this situation, the social worker's feelings and needs are all self-oriented. There is no place in this instance for consideration of the emotional needs of the patient. In such a circumstance, the following is an example of what can be expected in the patient/social worker relationship.

Social worker -	Hi
Patient -	Hello
Social worker -	I am (identifies self by name and profession.)
	I just came by to see if there is something we can do for you.
Patient -	No. I don't think so.
Social worker -	Well, if there is, just let us know.
Patient -	Thanks for stopping by
Social worker (smiles)	You're welcome. (exits)

The social worker leaves hastily knowing as does the patient that could very well be the last time they will see each other. The burden of establishing a relationship has been placed on the patient. "If you need anything...just let us know." The social worker can justify the effort made. "I asked if he needed anything. He said no. What else was there to do but leave?"

The same situation with the same people involved could

140

turn out quite differently: The social worker might experience the same initial feelings of discomfort already described but with two important exceptions: appreciation rather than anger that the physician not only recognized a common patient need (depression) but referred the patient for emotional support, and the final resolve would be to establish a therapeutic relationship with a person who is experiencing emotional pain rather than "getting it over as quickly as possible." In this way, the effort is patient oriented rather than self-oriented. Such an approach might be evidenced as follows:

Social worker -	Hi
Patient -	Hello
Social worker -	I am (identifies self by name and profession and states reason for coming by, i.e. to find out if there is anything that I can do to help you.)
Patient -	No, I don't think so.
Social worker -	Do you feel like talking?
Patient -	About what?
Social worker -	Anything
Patient -	No, I don't think so.
Social worker -	Well, I'm here whenever you need me. I work on this ward and two others, so you'll be seeing me almost every day.
Patient -	What do social workers do?
Social worker -	Oh, we help patients to work out their problems.
Patient -	Bet you can't help me work mine out.
Social worker -	Well, I'd like to try.
Patient -	How long have you been working here?
Social worker -	(tells him)
Patient -	You like it?
Social worker -	(tells him)
Patient -	Wish I could get out of here and go back to work.
Social worker -	What kind of work do you do?
Patient -	I paint houses.

This scenario is designed to illustrate the difference between what a caretaker and a terminal patient might talk about initially and what might be imagined. This example sets the tone and opportunity for the establishment of a patient/practitioner relationship building on the premise that the focus and purpose will be therapeutic. It is intentional rather than accidental that such relationships are established. It is the skill of the caretaker that sets the tone of the conversation. It is the planned focus of the intervention that assures the likelihood that rapport would be established and a therapeutic relationship sustained. Dr. Kubler-Ross has demonstrated that patients teach others what it is like to be dying: how they feel about it; what they experience in terms of fears, doubts and hopes. Practitioners who view terminal patients as people and relate to them on a human-to-human level enable the patients to teach us what their needs are and how we can meet those needs.

In the second example it is obvious that the patient and social worker are talking with each other. Without prior notice it would not be evident that the patient is terminal. Notice too, however, that the verbal exchange is purposeful; it flows in natural sequence and the patient is beginning to reach out to the social worker when he refers to "wishing to get out and to go back to work." He is testing the worker for support. The worker is aware and does not rush in to provide false assurance. The relationship is developing along therapeutic lines as intended and the social worker is showing no unmet needs of her own to force the progress of the relationship. When the patient is ready to talk about dying he will let the therapist know in both direct and subtle terms. The therapist, whether social worker, nurse, or any health care worker needs to be prepared to be supportive by learning to listen to what the patient says, to what is implied, and to what needs are being presented at any given time.

The practitioner learns to meet the patient where the patient is emotionally, and this can change from day to day. Patients do not look to therapists for answers to all their questions. They do hope, however, that caretakers are aware of their emotional needs and are able to stand by in a supportive manner, to respond in a way that is honestly human.

The social worker in the case of Mr. Eli is now in a position to begin to help the patient, and to meet and help the mother who will frequently visit her son during the next six months or so that he will live. The worker can serve as faciliatator to help guide them through the process of grief and in setting their affairs in order. Just as the patient will make known his needs, so will survivors who feel that strong support is available to them. An important aspect in terminal care is that the team must rely on team effort in good terminal care. No one person on staff should attempt to be all things to any patient or family. The strength of effectiveness in terminal care is in sharing. It is therapeutic for caretakers and insures consistency in treatment for the patients.

Specific needs of terminal patients include:
(1) opportunity to cope with the trauma of facing death.
(2) guidance and support in coping with the stresses imposed on their families.
(3) supportive intervention to help them to adjust to hospitalization.
(4) help in accepting gradual social losses: their jobs; their independence; everything as they have known it in life.
(5) assistance in working out solutions to financial problems.
(6) referrals for legal assistance.
(7) support in day by day living with a terminal condition.
(8) support to maintain dignity, individuality and self esteem.
(9) support and encouragement to express thoughts and emotions.
(10) the right to be involved in their own treatment plans and decisions.
(11) the right to be informed
(12) support and understanding of the trauma associated with body image, physical deterioration and the effects of this on the patient and his family.

Health care practitioners will be able to evaluate their own therapeutic effectiveness if they adhere to their own unique personalities in the helping relationship. With experience in the process of their own personal growth and development, they will come to know when they are relating to the patient as a person.

This hypothetical situation may be used as a model to help you initiate similar situations in role playing exercises. Problems involving patients, families and staff in any combination may be selected to demonstrate dynamics, attitudes, and particular needs that exist in terminal care for patients and families as well as staff.

Exercise Three

Working with dying patients in therapeutic ways is not possible without developing insight into the frightening feelings that these patients experience. Patients can tell you that they are afraid or that they have regrets about what is happening to them, but you will not be able to fully appreciate what they are feeling unless you have some insight into what it must feel like to face one's own death. The imminence of death forces a person into the reality of the situation. If you can relate to the increase in the rate of our own heart beat; if you can appreciate the body tension that you experienced during Exercises One and Two, you will only have glimpsed a minute part of the emotional pain experienced by people who are in the actual process of dying.

Terminal patients who finally accept death with peace have been through deep emotional traumas that we can only imagine before they reach a point of acceptance. In order to help them, we need an established basis of identification with what their feelings must be.

Without the ability for empathy, people who work with dying patients are embarrassed to discover that they don't know what to do or say when a dying person reaches out to them for comfort. We feel inadequate when we are unable to relate to the feelings that a dying person is experiencing. We are therapeutically ineffective when our own personal fears and feelings prevent us from working with people who are dying in a supportive manner that encourages and allows them to mobilize their own inherent strengths.

A better understanding of your own gut-level feelings will help you to become aware of what terminal patients mean by what they say or do not say. Patients who are dying have never rehearsed the role of dying. They have no guidelines to follow. They do not know what is expected of them and can find themselves embarrassed by the ways in which they try to cope. Dying patients also do not know what to expect from staff, but they do hope that caretakers have something special to offer them. Caretakers who understand the dynamics of what may be happening between themselves and terminal patients in terms of mutual emotional needs, will be better able to give therapeutic care to dying patients. Terminal patients, in turn, support the practitioners by allowing them to grow through the experience of sharing their ultimate experience in the process of dying.

Exercise Three is designed to help you gain insight into what your feelings are when you are confronted with a dying person who is willing to share his or her feelings about dying with you. The object is to recognize your conscious awareness of what you feel: where you feel it; when you feel it; why you feel it; and how you handle your feelings in relation to what a dying person may be asking of you. It is a skill you can, with effort, learn; a skill that will be beneficial to you in various ways and therapeutically supportive to people who are traumatized by the fact that they are dying.

Role Playing Situations

1. Two people sit facing each other. One is the patient; the other player is the practitioner. The patient may represent a child or adult of any age. The practitioner may be of any discipline, i.e. physician, nurse, social worker, chaplain, or whatever.

The Role: A patient: (1) Is aware of his/her terminal condition.
(2) Realizes he/she is going to die.
(3) Is very frightened.
(4) Expresses fear of dying.

The Role: The practitioner responds according to what his/her own perception of what the patient's emotional needs are.
Discussion: Following the role playing — which is terminated by either player or group leader — the players are advised to "get out of role and return to a healthy state." This can be done by asking the players to close their eyes and gently leave behind the role they just assumed; to be themselves again. The group then discusses the dynamics and feelings and offer suggestions according to their perceptions of the "situations" and how they might be handled in other ways. This procedure is applied with each of the following situations. Each exercise requires a practitioner to offer therapeutic support. Each case represents a terminal illness.

2. *The Role:* A father: (1) has been told that his son is terminal.
   (2) feels helpless.
   (3) is dissappointed; had great plans for the future.
   (4) is angry.
   (5) feels he is being punished.

3. *The Role:* A Patient (1) feels neglected by staff.
   (2) wonders why staff is avoiding him/her.
   (3) wants answers to "what is wrong with me?"
   (4) suspects condition may be terminal.

4. *The Role: A wife:* (1) telephones head nurse (almost) every hour on the hour for reports on husband's condition.
   (2) Visits husband infrequently because she is "afraid she might cry and upset him."
   (3) does not want husband to know that she knows he is terminal.

5. *The Role: A Patient:* (1) is upset at being hospitalized.
   (2) is worried about inability to continue working.
   (3) is anxious about mortgage and financial support of family.
   (4) is worried about cost of hospitalization.
   (5) is afraid of being helpless.
   (6) is unable to express fear of dying.
   (7) is determined not to die.
   (8) is convinced the diagnosis is wrong.

6. *The Role:* A Patient: (1) Why me? is all that he verbalizes.
   (2) Is unable to move beyond this point.

7. *The Role:* A Patient: (1) Is upset because a patient in the same room just died.
   (2) Is afraid he/she will also die.

(3) Asks the nurse what happened to cause the roomates death.

(4) Asks to be moved to a different room.

The point of these exercises is to allow participants to reflect on the question "what would you do for these patients in these circumstances?" and proceed to seek solutions in therapeutic ways. You may construct your own role playing exercises according to your own learning needs.

We believe that one must have a philosophy of life in terms of where do we as humans fit into this vast universe and how do we as humans relate to each other in circumstances of life and death. Through the process of role playing, one does reveal the essence of his being to others while simultaneously helping himself to get in touch with feelings about who he is and what he is all about in a given situation.

True learning does not occur without pain. All growth is painful. Growth is relinquishing the security of the known and risking the uncertainties of the unknown. Role playing to enhance proficiency in terminal care is only one beginning. But, as Leo F. Buscaglia writes in his book on *Personhood,* 'Like the spider, there are those of us who refuse to stop spinning, even when it would appear to be far more sophisticated to be without hope.'"[7]

THE RIGHTS OF TERMINAL PATIENTS

A patient is admitted for hospital care because he is afflicted with disease. He may be in pain. We can be sure of one thing, and that is that he enters the facility with great apprehension that involves his total life. There is the fear that he will die. He has limited information about his illness. No one has told him, but he is afraid he has cancer. What will happen to him now? What about his job? His bills? His family? This man has always been in control of his life situations. He has been the strong dependable person upon whom other people could lean. And now here he is in the awful position of having to depend upon everyone for everything. This self-sufficient, take charge, productive individual is in the stressful situation of having to share information about such personal things as his toilet habits with

147

strangers. He is having his body manipulated and handled by other people; he is being served food according to someone else's timetable and choice of menu. He is in a state of helplessness. He is in your hands; and you must provide for his needs. He has lost control even over the most "insignificant" aspects of his life. Things that he has taken for granted for years such as when to get up, when to urinate, when to turn over and when to eat are no longer his independent choices. These are but a few of the personal choices that are no longer a patient's decision to make. It is enough to short-circuit the brain of anyone. Is there any wonder that this patient is angry?

It is important that you recognize, first of all, that this frightened lonely person has every right to be angry. It is important to realize that he is not angry specifically at you. He is confused and afraid of many things. If he strikes out in verbally abusive ways, it is in retaliation at the turn his life has taken. Unless you realize that at the outset, human nature will lead you to respond from your visceral feelings of negative emotions and you will unwittingly become a part of the patient's problems rather than a positive agent for change in his adjustment to his unfortunate situation.

The following items are included here to help you become aware of some of the needs that terminal patients have. Try to associate yourself with these needs and think of yourself in terms of how you can be helpful in each area of the patient's concerns. Make a conscious effort to identify with each of the items from the terminal patient's point of view and see how well you are able to identify with these needs and the basic rights of every terminal patient.

THE DYING PERSON'S BILL OF RIGHTS

1. I have the right to be treated as a living being until I die.
2. I have the right to maintain a sense of hopefulness, however changing its focus may be.
3. I have the right to be cared for by those who can maintain a sense of hopefulness, however changing this might be.
4. I have the right to express my feelings and emotions about my approaching death in my own way.
5. I have the right to participate in decisions concerning my own case.

148

6. I have the right to expect continuing medical and nursing attention even though "cure" goals must be changed to "comfort goals."
7. I have the right not to die alone.
8. I have the right to be free from pain.
9. I have the right to have my questions answered honestly.
10. I have the right not to be deceived.
11. I have the right to have help from and for my family in accepting my death.
12. I have the right to die in peace and dignity.
13. I have the right to retain my individuality and not be judged for my decisions, which may be contrary to the beliefs of others.
14. I have the right to discuss and enlarge my religious and/or spiritual experiences, regardless of what they may mean to others.
15. I have the right to expect that the sanctity of the human body will be respected after death.
16. I have the right to be cared for by caring, sensitive, knowledgeable people who will attempt to understand my needs and be able to gain some satisfaction in helping me face my death."[8]

Terminal care that is emotionally curative is characterized by individual and team approaches that take into account the fact that the patients require attention from staff focused on both the physical and the mental aspects of their illness. Efforts toward physical treatment will be enhanced if the patient is less worried about the social and financial problems caused by his illness. Patients can be relieved of these worries, onsofar as possible, to become more involved in the medical protocol of their treatment and in coping with the process of dying.

Think of yourself in a situation that is an oversimplification of the problems stated here, but one to which you can more readily relate. Imagine, for example, that final exams will take place this week. You have studied hard and prepared yourself to pass the tests. You are excitedly looking forward to graduating this year. You have worked very hard to earn your degrees and your family is preparing to witness this great moment. Your thesis is being typed in its final form. After passing exams, submission of the thesis is your last major requirement for graduation. You will pick it up from the typist today after class. The balance due is two hundred dollars. You lose your wallet. You cannot replace the money. The typist will not release the thesis without full payment. Your education has been a financial burden to your family. How can you call home and say that you lost the money they sent for your thesis preparation? You are not only panic-stricken at losing the money, you are now in the situation of taking final exams under extremely stressful conditions. How will this situation affect you?

Now imagine that you find your wallet on Friday and the money is intact. The exams are scheduled for the following Tuesday. Imagine the difference in your feelings and the approach that you will take in facing those exams. You are now able to relate to the challenge of passing. You are still in a position to hope that your best effort will be good enough.

In terminal care, unalleviated emotional stress is a significant barrier to a person's physical responsiveness to medical care. Finding the wallet is helpful to the student in terms of passing final examinations the same way as finding a friend on the staff is therapeutic to a terminal patient who is experiencing great stress while trying to maintain hope of recovery. When the practitioner's behavior toward the patient is supportive, the patient becomes unconsciously aware that he is liked, respected, and protected. It is therapy of this calibre that allows the patient the freedom to make more positive evaluations of himself, his behavior, and adjustments to his environment and situation. With other choices relinquished, the patient again is free to become an individual with the responsibility to choose his behavior in coping with his situation.

We are always experiencing some form of death in life. And each life situation helps us to mature. The practitioners who have matured from such life situations will be sensitive to the patients who reach out to their compassion. These are the moments in terminal care when two lives merge and each is unalterably changed.

> Give sorrow words; the grief that does not speak
> Whispers the o'er fraught heart, and bids it break.[9]
>
> —Shakespeare, MacBeth

ON HELPING EACH OTHER

We think about death even when we do not speak of it. We tend to see ourselves in a perpetual state of permanence. It is somehow easier for us to see ourselves as exempt from death and easier yet to see others as being susceptible to dying. This paradox would be perhaps more plausible if this death-denying statement guaranteed that since you are going to die and "I am immortal," I shall be there to help you when you are experiencing your terminal illness. But in reality, is this what really happens?

For the purpose of introspection, imagine that you are well and happy and that a colleague is dying. How would you reach out to him? How well would you be able to sustain a relationship with him through his protracted illness? What fears and feelings would interfere?

In order to help you get in touch with your own feelings about such possibilities as these, reflect on the following example of what it feels like.

DEATH IN THE FIRST PERSON

Anonymous

I am a student nurse. I am dying. I write this to you who are, and will become nurses in the hope that by my sharing feelings with you, you may someday be better able to help those who share my experience.

I'm out of the hospital now - perhaps for a month, for six months, perhaps for a year ... but no one likes to talk about such things. In fact, no one likes to talk about much at all. Nursing must be advancing, but I wish it would hurry. We're taught not to be overly cheery now, to omit the "Everything's fine" routine, and we have done pretty well. But now one is left in a lonely silent void. With the protective "fine, fine" gone, the staff is left with only their own vulnerability and fear. The dying patient is not yet seen as a person and thus cannot be communicatred with as such. He is a symbol of what every human fears and what we each know, at least academically, that we too must someday face. What did they say in psychiatric nursing about meeting pathology with pathology to the detriment of both patient and nurse? And there was a lot about knowing one's own feelings before you

151

could help another with his. How true.

But for me, fear is today and dying is now. You slip in and out of my room, give me medications and check my blood pressure. Is it because I am a student nurse myself, or just a human being, that I sense your fright? And your fear enhances mine. Why are you afraid? I am the one who is dying!

I know, you feel insecure, don't know what to say, don't know what to do. But please believe me, if you care, you can't go wrong. Just admit that you care. That is really what we search for. We may ask for why's and wherefore's but we don't really expect answers. Don't run away ... wait ... all I want to know is that there will be someone to hold my hand when I need it. I am afraid. Death may get to be a routine to you, but it is new to me. You may not see me as unique, but I've never died before. To me, once is pretty unique!

You whisper about my youth, but when one is dying, is he really so young anymore? I have lots I wish we could talk about. It really would not take much more of your time because you are in here quite a bit anyway.

If only we could be honest, both admit of our fears, touch one another. If you really care, would you lose so much of your valuable professionalism if you even cried with me? Just person to person? Then, it might not be so hard to die ... in a hospital ... with friends close by.

REFERENCES

1. *Successful Supervisor: A Bulletin of Ideas and Inspiration For Those Who Manage People*, Dartnell Corporation, Chicago, U.S.A., 1979.
2. Frost, Robert, "Stopping By Woods On A Snowy Evening", *Modern American Poetry/Modern British Poetry*, Edited by Louis Untermeyer, Harcourt Brace & Co., N.Y., 1919.
3. Shubin, Seymour, B.S., "Burnout," *Nursing*, Vol. 8, No. 7, July, 1978.
4. Shubin, Seymour, B.S., "Burnout," *Nursing*, Vol. 8, No. 7, July, 1978.
5. McAleenan, John, "A Time To Live and A Time to Die," *St. Petersburg Times*, St. Petersburg, Florida, November 14, 1976.
6. Weisman, Avery D., M.D., *On Dying and Denying: A Psychiatric Study of Terminology*, Harvard Medical School, 1972.
7. Buscaglia, Leo, *Personhood*, Charles B. Slack, Inc., Thorofare, New Jersey.
8. Ann Lander's Column, *St. Petersburg Times*, St. Petersburg, Florida, September, 1978.
9. Shakespeare, William, *Macbeth.*

PART VII

EPILOGUE

A great deal of talent is lost in the world from want of little courage. Every day send to their graves obscure men whom timidity prevented from making a first effort; who

if they could have been induced to begin, would have in all probability gone great lengths in the career of same.

The fact is that to do anything in the world worth doing we must not stand back shivering and thinking of the cold and danger but jump in and scramble through as well as we can.[1]

—Richard Cardinal Cushing

EPILOGUE

We believe that the material included in this book contains some of the things that practitioners in terminal care need to know. This book, therefore, is directed toward the special needs of people who are involved in the delivery of health services as well as the general public who question the meaning of death and who struggle to handle their own emotional problems when a loved one dies and when confronted with their own deaths.

This particular life is all that we know, and living it to the fullest is the only way to become what you alone can become. The process of becoming is really what *Learning to Say Goodbye* is all about. In terminal care, the continuum contains two major components. At one end of the continuum we find needs of terminal patients that practitioners are challenged to meet. At the other end of the continuum we find, too frequently, staff burnout. Somewhere in between lies the tragedy of unmet needs that encompasses both patients and staffs where these conditions are allowed to exist.

Robert Veringa, Associate Dean of the School of Public Health at the University of Minnesota, tells us that burn out "includes feelings that your job no longer holds excitement, risk or reward."[2] In terminal care, in order to prevent burn out, there must be the excitement that comes in the realization that there is support for the risks that are inherent in this highly sensitive area of health care; and that rewards are forthcoming for having made the effort.

Burn out comes, he says to people who feel that they "must succeed even if it kills them."[3] In terminal care this can be a self-fulfilling prophecy for those few practitioners who are dedicated to alleviating the stresses of other people at their own expense. What this means is that no man is an island. Teamwork in terminal care, together with sufficient training, will lessen the emotional burdens to practitioners who are committed to their work.

Professional practitioners who prevent burn out in

themselves are caretakers who have learned that it is possible to give unselfishly but have learned to develop certain systems of support from related sources that sustain them and alleviate the stresses of their day to day activities. Creative terminal care is sharing of responsibilities and having the ability to function and grow.

It is our hope that the readers will come to know the importance of touching each other's lives significantly.

It is our intention that the ending of this book shall facilitate the beginning for some of its readers. Herbert Otto says it best: "We are all functioning at a small fraction of our capacity to live fully in its total meaning of loving, caring, creating and adventuring. Consequently, the actualizing of our potential can become the most exciting adventure of our lifetime."[16]

> *I don't know what your destiny will be, but one thing I know:*
> *The only ones among you who will really be happy are those who have sought and found how to serve.*[17]
>
> — *Albert Schweitzer*

REFERENCES

1. Cushing, Cardinal Richard.
2. Veringa, Robert, Associate Dean, School of Public Health, University of Minnesota.
3. Veringa, Robert, Associate Dean, School of Public Health, University of Minnesota
4. Otto, Herbert, "Criteria for Assessing Family Strength." *Family Process* 2:329-338 September, 1963.
5. Albert Schweitzer, *Successful Supervisor: A Bulletin of Ideas and Inspiration For Those Who Manage People,* Dartnell Corporation, Chicago, U.S.A., 1979.

SUGGESTED READINGS

Alsop, Stewart, *Stay of Execution*, J.B. Lippincott Co., Phila., and New York, 1973.

Aries, Philippe, *Western Attitudes Toward Death*, The John Hopkins University Press, Baltimore and London, 1974.

Alsenberg, Ruth B. and Kastenbaum, Ph.D., Robert, *The Psychology of Death*, Springer, New York, 1972.

Austin, Mary, *Experience Facing Death*, Indianapolis, 1931.

Bailey, Ralph, *For Everything A Season*, Hawthorne Books, Inc., New York, 1975.

Bayley, Joseph, *The View From A Hearse*, David C. Cook Co., Elgin, Ill., 1969.

Becker, Ernest, *The Denial of Death*, Free Press, New York, 1975.

Benton, Richard G. *Death and Dying*, Van Nostrand Reinhold, New York, 1978.

Bowers, M., et. al., *Counseling The Dying*, Thomas Nelson, New York, 1964.

Bowman, LeRoy, *The American Funeral, A Study in Guilt, Extravagance and Sublimity*, Public Affairs Press, Washington, D.C., 1959.

Bullmer, Kenneth, *The Art of Empathy, A Manual for Improving Accuracy of Interpersonal Perception,* Human Sciences, New York, 1975.

Caine, Lynn, *Widow*, Bantam Books, New York, 1974.

Colen, B.D. *Karen Ann Quinlan: Dying In The Age of Eternal Life*, Nash Publishing, New York, 1976.

Comfort, Alex, *The Nature of Human Nature*, Harper and Row Publishers, New York and Evanston, 1966.

Curran, Charles A., *Religious Values In Counseling and Psychotherapy*, Sheed and Ward, New York, 1969.

de Beauvior, Simone, *A Very Easy Death*, Warner Paperback, New York, 1973.

de Beauvior, Simone, *The Coming of Age*, Translated by Patrick O'Brien, G.P. Putnam Sons, New York, 1972.

Drummond, Eleanor, Ed.D., "Communication and Comfort For The Dying Patient," *Nursing Clinics of North America*, March 1970, pp. 55-63.

Ettinger, R. C. W., *The Prospect of Immortality*, Mac Fadden - Bartell, New York, 1964.

Feifel, Herman (ed.) *The Meaning of Death*, McGraw-Hill, New York, 1969.

Feifel, Herman (ed.) *New Meaning of Death*, McGraw-Hill, New York, 1977.

Glaser, B.G. and Ansolm Strauss, *Anguish: A Case History of A Dying Trajectory*, The Sociology Press, California, 1970.

Glaser, B.G., and Ansolm Strauss, *Time For Dying*, Aldine, Chicago, 1967.

Glick, Ira O., et al: *The First Year of Bereavement*, John Wiley & Sons, New York, 1974.

Greene, W. and S. Troiys (eds.), *The Patient, Death and the Family*, Charles Scribner's, New York, 1974.

Grinsell, Leslie V., Barrow, *Pyramid and Tomb: Ancient Burial Customs in Egypt, The Mediterranean and The British Isles*, Westview Press, Inc., Boulder, Colo. 1975.

Grollman, E. (ed.), *Concerning Death: A Practical Guide for the Living*, Beacon Press, Boston, 1974.

Grollman, E. (ed.), *Explaining Death to Children*, Beacon Press, Boston, 1969.

Haberstein, Robert and William Lamars, *Funeral Customs the World Over*, Bulfin Printers, 1963.

Herzog, Edgar, *Psyche and Death*, G.P. Putnam Sons, for the C. G. Jung Foundation for Analytical Psychology, New York, 1966.

Hick, John H., *Death and Eternal Life*, Harper and Row, New York, 1976.

Jonas, Dr. Doris, and Jonas, Dr. David, *Young Till We Die*, Coward, McCann and Geoghegan, Inc., New York, 1973.

Kastenbaum, Robert, Ph.D., *Death, Society, and Human Experience*, C.V. Mosby, St. Louis, 1977.

Kastenbaum, Robert, Ph.D., & Aisenberg, Ruth, *The Psychology of Death*, Springer Publishing Co., Inc., New York, 1972.

Keleman, Stanley, *Living Your Dying*, Random House, New York, 1974.

Kubler-Ross, Elisabeth, M.D., *Death, the Final Stage of Growth*, Prentice-Hall, Englewood Cliffs, 1975.

Kubler-Ross, Elisabeth, M.D., *On Death and Dying*, Mac-Millan, New York, 1969.

Kubler-Ross, Elisabeth, M.D., *Questions and Answers on Death and Dying*, MacMillan, New York, 1974.

Kutscher, A.H. (ed.) *Death and Bereavement*, C. C. Thomas, Springfield, 1969.

Lewis, C.S., *A Grief Observed*, Seabury Press, New York, 1963.

Moody, R. *Life After Life*, Bantam Books, New York, 1976.

Moody, Virginia,*Ho For Heaven*, E. P. Dutton & Co., Inc., New York, 1946.

Moustakas, C.E., *Loneliness*, Prentice-Hall, Inc., Englewood Cliffs, N.J., 1961.

Menninger, Karl, with the collaboration of Jeanetta Lyle Menninger, *Love Against Hate*, Harcourt Brace & Co., New York, 1942.

Nowell, R. *What A Modern Catholic Believes About Death*, Thomas Moore Press, Chicago, 1972.

Parks, Colin Murray, *Bereavement*, International Universities Press, New York, 1972.

Pearson, Linnea and Ruth B. Purtillo, *Separate Paths - Why People End Their Lives*, Harper and Row, New York, 1977.

Reed, Elizabeth L., *Helping Children With the Mystery of Death*, Abingdon Press, Nashville and New York, 1970.

Riemer, Jack, *Jewish Reflections On Death*, Schecken Books, New York, 1972.

Rudolph, Marguerita, *Should The Children Know? Encounters With Death in the Lives of Children*, Schocken Books - New York, 1978.

Russell, Ruth O., *Freedom To Die: Moral and Legal Aspects of Euthanasia*, Human Sciences Press, A Division of Behavioral Publications, Inc., New York, 1975.

Schneidman, Edwin S., *Deaths of Man*, Penguin Books, Baltimore, 1974.

Sheehy, Gail, Passages: *Predictable Crises of Adult Life*, E. P. Dutton & Co., Inc., New York, 1974.

Silverstone, Barbara and Hyman, Helen Kandel, *You and Your Aging Parents*, Pantheon Books, New York, 1976.

Spraggett, Allen, *The Case of Immortality: The Story of Life After Death* New American Library/Times Mirror, New York, 1974.

Toynbee, Arthur, Koestter, Arthur and others (contributions) *Life After Life*, McGraw-Hill Book Co., New York, St. Louis, San Francisco, 1976.

Weissman, Avery D., *The Psychological Autopsy, A Study of the Terminal Phase of Life*, Human Sciences, New York, 1972.

Wilson, Jerry B., *Death By Decision*, Westminster Press, Phila., 1975.

About the Authors

Rosalie Peck   Charlotte Stefanics

Rosalie Peck, M.S.W., A.C.S.W., is a native of St. Petersburg, Florida. She holds a Master's degree in social work from Atlanta University School of Social Work, Atlanta, Georgia. Ms. Peck is a Cum Laude graduate of Bethune-Cookman College, Daytona Beach, Florida, where she received the Bachelor of Arts degree in Sociology. She is a former resident of Nassau, Bahamas, and has practiced social work extensively in various settings from Michigan to California to Florida, where she now resides. She is an accomplished speaker, who serves as consultant on Living and Dying; conducts workshops and presents papers on the subject in various parts of the United States. Ms. Peck is a prolific writer. Learning To Say Good-Bye is her first publication.

Dr. Charlotte Stefanics, a psychiatric-mental health clinical nurse specialist, has an extensive and impressive background in the areas of nursing and mental health in various hospital settings from New York City to Florida. She recently returned from China where she had been invited for a nursing exchange program. She is an active speaker and writer.